HOW TO BE AN
OVERCOMER

LIVE THE ABUNDANT LIFE

HOW TO BE AN OVERCOMER

LIVE THE ABUNDANT LIFE

Dale Shannon

Fulfill Your Dream
www.fulfillyourdream.org

HOW TO BE AN OVERCOMER
LIVE THE ABUNDANT LIFE

Copyright © 2018 Dale Shannon

All rights reserved. No part of this publication may be reproduced, distributed, or transmitted in any form or by any means, including photocopying, recording, or other electronic or mechanical methods, without the prior written permission of the publisher, except in the case of brief quotations embodied in critical reviews and certain other noncommercial uses permitted by copyright law. For permission requests, contact the author at the web address below:

Fulfill Your Dream
Manhattan Beach, CA 90266
www.fulfillyourdream.org

Scripture taken from the New King James Version®. Copyright © 1982 by Thomas Nelson. Used by permission. All rights reserved

Scripture quotations taken from the New American Standard Bible® (NASB), Copyright © 1960, 1962, 1963, 1968, 1971, 1972, 1973, 1975, 1977, 1995 by The Lockman Foundation Used by permission. www.Lockman.org

Scripture taken from the Holy Bible, NEW INTERNATIONAL VERSION®, NIV® Copyright © 1973, 1978, 1984, 2011 by Biblica, Inc.® Used by permission. All rights reserved worldwide.

Scripture quotations marked TPT are from The Passion Translation®. Copyright © 2017, 2018 by Passion & Fire Ministries, Inc. Used by permission. All rights reserved. ThePassionTranslation.com.

Scripture quotations from The Authorized (King James) Version. Rights in the Authorized Version in the United Kingdom are vested in the Crown. Reproduced by permission of the Crown's patentee, Cambridge University Press

Italics in Scripture quotations have been added by the author for emphasis.

Copy Editor, Interior Layout and Formatting: Tammie Pelletier
Cover and Interior Design and Layout: Christian Wetzel

ISBN: 1-7329236-0-4
ISBN-13: 978-1-7329236-0-7

OTHER BOOKS BY DALE SHANNON:

Understanding Dreams Heals the Soul

Fulfill Your Dream and Destiny

Fulfill Your Dream by Life Purpose Coaching

To contact the author about speaking at your conference or church, please go to:

Fulfill Your Dream
Manhattan Beach, CA 90266
www.fulfillyourdream.org

ENDORSEMENTS

Dale Shannon has spent uncounted hours helping to nurture people into not only a healing journey, but how to grab hold of their identity and live out a fully empowered life. She is an educator and a coach herself and has created resources that can help you bypass years of therapy, coaching, and process. This tool holds you by the hand and causes you to come into the right frame of mind for a real growth experience. Dale has always had a heart to sacrificially nurture others and writing is a natural progression to this. You are going to want to get her resources for yourself and your family! Too many people are stuck thinking of life as overly complex but when you have a master coach and mentor imparting life lessons and wisdom through well-crafted books you will enjoy a simplified journey into the real and authentic you. I praise what Dale has done and who she is, and I highly recommend her materials to you.

Shawn Bolz
Author of Translating God, Modern Prophets, and God Secrets
www.bolzministries.com

How to Be an Overcomer is a valuable handbook for both seasoned intercessors and those new to prayer. This resource is for those desiring to grow in their relationship with God and establish kingdom transformation and reformation to the earth. Dale Shannon has discovered the difference between praying as a beggar and praying as a bride. She shares with us transformative keys she has learned as a prayer minister, life coach, and educator that will truly empower you to live life to the fullest by bringing restoration to people and to land. Such keys include discernment training, breaking generational curses, priestly heavenly courtroom prayer, overcoming trauma, core alignment, putting on the mind of Christ, and restoring the land. As Dale has traveled with us to nations, I've witnessed her compassion and authority as she has prayed over regions, and for individuals. Dale has a heart to bring kingdom restoration to the earth. I highly recommend both Dale and her materials to you.

Ann Tubbs
HIM Missions Apostle

I do not know what circumstances brought Dale Shannon to our Aslan's Place schools in 2005 but it soon became clear that the student would become one of our teachers. For many years and in many countries, Dale attended our schools and received groundbreaking revelation that propelled Aslan's Place into many new areas of healing. Dale has continued to grow as she hears from the Lord and has written a new book, How to Be an Overcomer, that will help you bring healing to not only yourself but others. I like what John Wimber said, "You come to ministry with an empty toolbox being willing to allow the Holy Spirit to put into that toolbox the tools that you need for the moment." How To Be An Overcomer is definitely a book you would like to have available in your toolbox.

Paul L. Cox
Aslan's Place, Apple Valley, CA

Over the years, Shirley and I have known Dale as not only a prolific intercessor, but also possessing a unique ability to teach people how to step into freedom and fullness in their destiny. Her husband Doug, and Dale are great friends, and I am sure you will not only be blessed - but changed - when you read her amazing biblical insights and personal revelation regarding inner healing, discernment, restoration as well as an understanding of the heavenly courts.

Bon Appetit!

Charlie Robinson
Revival Canada Ministries

TABLE OF CONTENTS

	ACKNOWLEDGEMENTS	11
	INTRODUCTION	13
Chapter 1	TRI-PART BEINGS	15
Chapter 2	DISCERNMENT OF GOOD AND EVIL	19
Chapter 3	SEPARATION OF SOUL AND SPIRIT	27
Chapter 4	CLEANSING SPIRIT, SOUL, BODY GATES	31
Chapter 5	COVENANT, EXCHANGES, TRADING	33
Chapter 6	SIN AND GENERATIONAL CURSES	37
Chapter 7	TRADING FLOORS	39
Chapter 8	TREASURES OF DARKNESS PROPHETIC WORD	43
Chapter 9	PRIESTHOOD PRAYER	45
Chapter 10	HEAVENLY COURTROOM PRAYER PROTOCOL	51
Chapter 11	DIVINE EXCHANGE	53
Chapter 12	PRAYER TO BECOME A LIVING SACRIFICE	55
Chapter 13	PRAYER TO ESTABLISH GOD'S NEW FOUNDATION	57
Chapter 14	OVERCOMING TRAUMA AND BROKENNESS	61
Chapter 15	CORE ALIGNMENT TOOL: PICTURE IN PICTURE PIP	65
Chapter 16	BECOMING AN OVERCOMER	69
Chapter 17	PROMISES TO OVERCOMERS	71
Chapter 18	HOW TO OVERCOME	77
Chapter 19	PUTTING ON THE MIND OF CHRIST	79
Chapter 20	TAKING TERRITORY	83
Chapter 21	PRAYER TO DISMANTLE DEFILED LAND	85
	ABOUT THE AUTHOR	89

ACKNOWLEDGMENTS

I want to thank my husband, Doug Shannon, for his love, encouragement, and support in writing this book.

I want to thank all my leaders and mentors who saw something good in me and called it out. You know who you are, and I appreciate every encouraging word. Thanks especially to Shawn Bolz, Charlie Robinson, and Dr. Paul Cox for your friendship, inspiration and encouragement.

I want to thank the hundreds of clients I've ministered to personally and have had the privilege of coaching you to transform your thinking, set goals and achieve your heart's desire. Through you, the Lord has taught me much about healing of the soul, renewing the mind, and living the ascended life. I bless you all.

I want to thank the prophetic teams and small groups I have led throughout the years. Thank you for teaching me through your God encounters. You are awesome and I believe in you.

I want to thank most of all, my God, Holy Spirit and Lord Jesus, for loving me, teaching me and leading me in every step of writing this book.

INTRODUCTION

How to Be an Overcomer imparts significant keys to living the abundant life Jesus promised us in John 10:10. These transformative keys have been developed through my years of ministering, life coaching, and teaching people to be transformed from areas of being stuck to becoming whole, productive and free to fulfill their dreams and life purpose. Originally written to equip ministers of healing, *How to Be an Overcomer*, is for everyone who desires to overcome obstacles and fulfill their dreams. This resource coaches you to live the abundant life through discernment, becoming a priest, heavenly courtroom prayer, renewing the mind, and terraforming the land. My passion is to bring kingdom restoration to people and regions.

CHAPTER 1 TRI-PART BEINGS

Now may the God of peace Himself sanctify you completely; and may your whole spirit, soul, and body be preserved blameless at the coming of our Lord Jesus Christ.
(1 Thess. 5:23, NKJV)

Many believers today are not living the abundant life promised in John 10:10. Many are struggling with stress, depression, anxiety and are overwhelmed. Many are not living above their circumstances but instead are living defeated lives. Why is this when God has promised us an abundant life? Why is it that many are just trying to survive and keep their head above water?

The answer is that there is an unseen war going on for you to not reach your potential, or your God given destiny. There's a realm that most do not see of darkness and light. However, what is going on in the unseen realm can affect you mentally, emotionally, and physically.

You are a three part being: spirit, soul, and body. Few medical professionals and counselors understand the influences and interaction between the three dimensions. Before the fall in the garden in Eden, the spirit of man interacted with God daily, as man walked with God communing with God heart to heart. With the fall of man, the spirit imploded, going on the inside of the body. The soul has been the mediator between the spirit and the body. Instead of just treating or medicating symptomatic problems of the mind or body, we need to understand that there possibly could be root causes in the unseen realm, acting behind the scene that are influencing the mind and body.

In Ephesians 6:12, we learn that we are not fighting against the flesh, but against spiritual forces in the unseen realm.

> *"For our struggle is not against flesh and blood, but against the rulers, against the powers, against the world forces of this darkness, against the spiritual forces of wickedness in the heavenly places." (Eph. 6:12, NASB)*

In 2 Corinthians 5:17, we learn that we are new creatures in Christ; therefore our battles in life are not with our old natures. Though our flesh may be weak, it is no longer corrupt. The enemy works hard on deceiving you, so you don't know your authority as a child of God, capable of overcoming the onslaughts of lies and traps set by evil forces against your success. Instead of resisting the enemy, you may turn against yourself in self-sabotage believing the lies that you are worthless, defeated, and shouldn't even try to accomplish life goals, or the dreams God wrote on your scroll. Destructive cycles and patterns emerge holding you captive in your thoughts, words, actions, and habits. But through Jesus' death, the spirit of God has been imparted to set you free from the destructive cycles and patterns. My hope is that you will identify and break agreement with the deceptive lies of the enemy, and embrace the truth of Jesus Christ so you can become all that He has called you to be, free indeed. May you be filled with the Spirit of Truth and enlightenment as you glean from this material the liberty and fullness of all God has purposed for you.

I remember being a child in Memphis, having fun playing, swimming, and jumping off the diving board of the local swimming pool, when a smiling man approached me, and said, "I know who your Daddy is. You look just like him." I felt too embarrassed to answer, and jumped into the pool. But I still remember what this stranger said to me. We are created in God's image, and we are growing to look just like our Father God. Others, even the enemy, recognize who we are, yet we somehow don't. Not knowing who we are as children of the King of Kings leaves us vulnerable to the enemy. God is spirit, and as children procreated of God, we too are spirit beings. The enemy's deception is for us to forget and not know where we came from. We need to remember who we are, where we came from and who our Daddy is.

> *Then God said, "Let us make man in Our image, according to Our likeness; let them have dominion over the fish of the sea, over the birds of the air, and over the cattle, over all the earth and over every creeping thing that creeps on the earth." So God created man in His own image; in the image of God He created him; male and female He created them. (Gen. 1:26-27, NKJV)*

"Today class, we will explore our timelines," is what I heard as I was sitting in a Life Coaching Certification class. As we were to imagine our timelines, I was immediately caught up in a vision seeing myself with Father God in a heavenly place telling me it was time to come to earth. I saw my timeline differently from every other student in the class, because it was circular instead of linear. I knew I came from Father God and will return to Father God with a linear time on earth. I instantly knew that my beginning was with the Father as a spirit being. The revelation of being a spirit being instead of a human being changes how we interact with heaven. The perspective of being a spirit being engaging with the earthly realm is far different than the perspective of being a human being engaging with the heavenly realm.

God created man, male and female, to rule and have dominion over creation. Since man was created in the very image of God, whoever looked upon him would recognize God in him. Adam and Eve were able to commune with God daily, spirit to spirit as their human nature was covered with the glory of their own spirit, deposited by God. Adam's spirit and soul were cloaked in Christ in who were all the treasures of wisdom and knowledge.

> *That their hearts may be encouraged, being knit together in love, and attaining to all riches of the full assurance of understanding, to the knowledge of the mystery of God, both of the Father and of Christ, in whom are hidden all the treasures of wisdom and knowledge. (Col. 2:2-3, NKJV)*

Adam had intelligence, wisdom, knowledge and power to govern all creation. He was created to move in the natural and spiritual dimensions simultaneously. He was filled with the joy and love of the Father, and given free will of the soul.

When God made man in His image, He breathed life into him. For the spirit and flesh to communicate, the soul was created to mediate and give the spirit access to the body and the natural world. Originally, the soul reflected the spirit, reflecting God's glory, but then came the fall. Lucifer, a spiritual being, was a cherub who rebelled and exalted himself in his heart to be like God, and was cast down by God along with 1/3 of the angels (Isa. 14:12-15, Rev. 12:4, 9). He envied the sons of God, created in the image of God, possessing the very DNA of God; and coveted man's tripartite being, a created spirit living in a body and having a soul that relates to both the spiritual and the natural worlds. He desired the soul of man so he could have dominion over the earth, and with that desire he was effective in deceiving Eve.

CHAPTER 2
DISCERNMENT OF GOOD AND EVIL

But solid food belongs to those who are of full age, that is those who by reason of use have their senses exercised to discern both good and evil.
(Heb. 5:14, NKJV)

The church as a whole lacks discernment. We have been tossed by every wind of doctrine. We have thrown out the supernatural out of fear of being deceived because we don't know how to test the spirits. The new age has stolen the supernatural and run with it, while we, as spiritual beings have been asleep and allowed the supernatural to be stolen. We have allowed our children to be entertained by Harry Potter, believing white magic is good, dulling the senses of right and wrong. It's all because we don't know who we are, or the authority God has given to us. It was stolen from us generationally at the fall, but even though Christ Jesus got the authority back, we are unaware and our spirit man is still asleep.

When Jesus sent out his disciples, He gave these instructions:

> *"Behold, I send you out as sheep in the midst of wolves. Therefore be wise as serpents and harmless as doves. But be aware of men, for they will deliver you up to councils and scourge you in their synagogues." (Matt. 10:16, NKJV)*

Jesus is telling us to be wise, so we are not deceived. We are living in the last days, and the enemy knows his time is short. There's an increase of lies, and deception as the prince of the power of the air rules our airwaves and media. How do we stand in this battle of what is right and what is wrong?

> *Finally, be strong in the Lord and in the strength of His might. Put on the full armor of God, so that you will be able to stand firm against the schemes of the devil. For our struggle is not against flesh and blood, but against the rulers, against the powers, against the world forces of this darkness, against the spiritual forces of wickedness in the heavenly places. Therefore, take up the full armor of God, so that you will be able to resist in the evil day, and having done everything, to stand firm. Stand firm therefore, having girded your loins with truth, and having put on the breastplate of righteousness, and having shod your feet with the preparation of the gospel of peace; in addition to all, taking up the shield of faith with which you will be able to extinguish all the flaming arrows of the evil one. And take the helmet of salvation, and the sword of the Spirit, which is the word of God. (Eph. 6: 10-17, NASB)*

In the heat of this spiritual battle, we are called to stand. God has promised to equip us, and train us as we look to Him, our hope and strong tower. As we turn to Him, He will fight the battle for us.

> *And he said, "Listen, all Judah and the inhabitants of Jerusalem and King Jehoshaphat: thus says the Lord to you, Do not fear or be dismayed because of this great multitude, for the battle is not yours but God's." (2 Chron. 20:15, NASB)*

The gift of discernment is one of the nine gifts of the Holy Spirit listed in 1 Corinthians 12:10. We are to earnestly desire spiritual gifts. Earnestly desire means to lust after and to pursue. Discernment of spirits is the ability to determine between genuine revelation from God and that which is false. We are to test the spirits, and their fruit.

> *Beloved, do not believe every spirit, but test the spirits to see whether they are from God, because many false prophets have gone out into the world. By this you know the Spirit of God: every spirit that confesses that Jesus Christ has come in the flesh is from God; and every spirit that does not confess Jesus is not from God; this is the spirit of the antichrist, of which you have heard that it is coming, and now it is already in the world. You are from God, little children, and have overcome them; because greater is He who is in you than he who is in the world. (1 John 4:1-4, NASB)*

TWO TREES

God had said:

> *"But of the tree of the knowledge of good and evil you shall not eat, for in the day that you eat of it you shall surely die." (Gen. 2:17, NKJV)*

Then the serpent said to the woman, "You will not surely die. For God knows that in the day you eat of it your eyes will be opened, and you will be like God, knowing good and evil." (Gen. 3:4-5, NKJV)

The Tree of Life was the divine provision given so that man could live eternally in Paradise. On the other hand, the tree of the knowledge of good and evil would bring separation for man from his Father and his God. When Adam and Eve ate from this alternative tree, they died to their communion with God. Their spirit fell into a state of sleep and their soul, which had been covered by the splendor of their spirit, was left naked and condemned to death. The spirit of man, either alive or dead (asleep) determines the final destiny of the soul. At the fall, the spirit of man lost its dominion and ability to rule. The soul instead became the ruler governed by the knowledge and the wisdom of darkness.

Today, we see a lot of interest in the supernatural. The supernatural realm is just as real as the natural realm. We are spirit beings created to interact with the spirit realm. The problem is many go about entering into the supernatural realm through the tree of knowledge instead of through the Tree of Life. God gives gifts of revelation, but unless you are tuned to the Tree of Life, all you will get is information from the dark realm. Your revelation will be tainted and will only be information from the demonic network. Which spiritual frequency are you tuned to? To which tree is your satellite dish tuned? Is it the tree of life, the tree of knowledge of good and evil, or the tree of death?

TWO TREES SUMMARY

Tree of the Knowledge of Good and Evil – It is built on pride, to be like God. It brings death. The information comes from the demonic network.

Tree of Life – It is connected to Jesus. It brings life. Revelation comes from God.

Jesus is the 2nd Adam, and when he rose from the dead, He took back the keys and the authority to rule the earth that was handed over to Satan at the fall. Disconnect from the tree of knowledge of good and evil, so you can connect fully to the Tree of Life. Jesus is the Tree of Life. Jesus is the vine, and we are the branches that must abide in Him to bear good fruit (John 15:1-6).

HOW TO GROW IN THE GIFT OF DISCERNMENT

Train your senses; practice (Heb. 5:14). This is detailed later in this chapter. Ask God for discernment so you are not deceived. The nature of being deceived is that you don't know you are deceived. The Lord appeared to Solomon in a dream visitation.

> *At Gibeon the Lord appeared to Solomon in a dream by night; and God said, "Ask! What shall I give you?" "Therefore give to your servant an understanding heart to judge Your people, that I may discern between good and evil. For who is able to judge this great people of Yours?" (1 Kings 3:5, 9; NKJV)*

Solomon's answer in verse 9 should be the cry of our hearts. Solomon's answer pleased God Who delighted to give him what he requested and in addition God gave him riches, honor, peace with his enemies, and long life (1 Kings 3:10-15).

HOW TO DISCERN THE TRUE FROM THE FALSE

Test the words you hear and visions you get, to see if they line up with the Spirit of Truth, the Lord Jesus.

1. What is the spirit behind the words? Does it bring fear or love? God is love. There is no fear in love; but perfect love casts out fear, because fear involves torment. But he who fears has not been made perfect in love. (1 John 4:18, NKJV)
2. What is the fruit of the word? (Matt. 7:15-16) Does it bring encouragement or condemnation? Does it edify, exhort and comfort? Like Abraham you are called to be blessed and be a blessing to others. (Gen. 12:2; 1 Cor. 14:3)
3. Does this word conflict with scriptures? A true word will not violate scripture. (John 17:17)
4. Does this word represent God's nature, and the heart of God? (1 Cor. 13)
5. Do you and your wise counselors bear witness to the word?
6. Does the word come to pass?

Additionally, you can line up the content of the words you hear against the names of Satan and the names of the Holy Spirit.

Names of Satan:

Accuser
Adversary
Liar
Destroyer
Condemner
Thief
Murderer

Names of the Holy Spirit:

Edifier
Comforter
Teacher
Creator
Divine Lover
Healer
Giver of Life

TEST THE SOURCE FOR THE WORD

Self - It is born in meditation. It is a progression of building ideas, a consideration of things learned, selfish ambition, soulish, and carnal.

Satan - It is lofty speculation. It accuses, twists the truth, exalts self, and is prideful. The fruit is destruction, obstruction, negativity, fear, and/or hate.

God - It is sensed in the innermost being. The fruit is peace, truth, and love of God.

MATURE BELIEVERS DISCERN

We have much to say about this, but it is hard to make it clear to you because you no longer try to understand. In fact, though by this time you ought to be teachers, you need someone to teach you the elementary truths of God's word all over again. You need milk, not solid food! Anyone who lives on milk, being still an infant, is not acquainted with the teaching about righteousness. But solid food is for the mature, who by constant use have trained themselves to distinguish good from evil. (Heb. 5:11-14, NIV)

Have you noticed that you can walk into or drive into a new environment, and the atmosphere has seemingly changed? I enjoy riding my bike on the strand, and I can sense the atmosphere shift as I ride through different cities. As soon as I cross the border from one city to the next, bam! I sense the difference. Discernment is sensing through your five physical senses what is going on in the spiritual realm. Remember the unseen realm is more real than the seen realm.

I remember being in traditional church one Sunday, and the Lord showed me a vision of drinking milk. Later that day, I visited a different church for the first time, where the spirit was flowing, and the Lord showed me a vision of eating steak. This was a revelation to me since I had been taught that eating the meat was doing an exegetical study of the Greek and Hebrew language. But in actuality, eating the meat is discerning with your physical senses the spiritual realm. Discernment is described as a sensory rather than an intellectual process. I often see God smiling as He teaches me something new and enlightening for this teacher of the word. This new insight became my green light and starting point for valuing and engaging the spiritual realm. Later, I was fortunate to have a mentor of discernment training, Dr. Paul Cox.

The book of Hebrews says mature believers are ready for solid food by growing in discernment of good and evil. The mature are constantly training to distinguish good from evil. Discernment is not child's play. It is a mark of the mature Christian. According to 1 Corinthians 12:10, discernment is a spiritual gift. But as the writer of Hebrews clearly teaches, this gift must be developed by constant practice. Only then will discernment become a sharpened weapon of spiritual warfare. To enter into heavenly places, we need to have a pure heart.

Who may ascend into the hill of the Lord? Or who may stand in His holy place? He who has clean hands and a pure heart, who has not lifted up his soul to falsehood and has not sworn deceitfully. (Ps. 24:3-4, NASB)

Blessed are the pure in heart, for they shall see God. (Matt. 5:8, NASB)

To know God is to experience God (Yada Hebrew, Ginosko Greek). In order to experience God and to know God and His realm, we need to have a pure heart and know righteousness, so we aren't deceived and tossed by every wind of doctrine (Eph. 4:14). Discernment is essential for our maturity as believers. We can discern spiritual beings and spiritual things. You may see, hear, taste, smell, and feel. All of this is scriptural. In our western education, we've been taught to only value logic and not intuitive thinking. This is actually the difference between the Greek mindset and the Hebrew mindset. This is an area of growth for most of us to value what we are sensing.

In ministry, when I am praying for someone, I put on my discernment hat, and connect to the Lord. Keeping in mind, I don't always report to the receiver what I'm getting. The Lord can show us where the person is, and as we pray, we can sense things shifting. We ask God what He wants to do, and with their agreement, we break ungodly ties with the enemy, so they can be set free.

People discern differently, so there is no set dictionary for discernment. Discernment is not always fun. It's not fun to experience heavy witchcraft which can be pressure around the head, or a nauseous feeling. We'll each have stronger areas of discernment whether it be sight, hearing, feeling, tasting, smelling, or the 6th sense, knowing. It's good to compare with each other what we are getting. I've smelled sulfur as people are getting delivered and roses when the bridegroom enters a meeting. I've been in vivid visions of the tabernacle, and heard the Lord speak audibly, and angels speak audibly. I've seen and engaged with spiritual beings and the cloud of witnesses. Sometimes our knower goes off with a word of knowledge. As we grow in maturity, God equips us and releases His spiritual servants to protect us as we are sent into new territory and higher levels of spiritual authority.

Another not so fun part of discernment is that we can have the gift to make demons manifest. As an intercessor, I can be sitting next to a person and know that person is getting delivered. The intercessor shares in the sufferings of Jesus by being the vessel the demonic leaves (2 Cor. 1:5). For example, I do a lot of yawning when I pray for people. We take authority over the demonic, so the receiver does not have to manifest or throw up, but the demonic will leave quietly and go to where Jesus sends it.

PRACTICE

1. Find a partner. One will be the intercessor and the other receives.
2. Ask the Lord to give you discernment as you do a body scan of your partner.
3. Ask the Lord to show you what is coming against your partner. You may sense a knife in your partner's back, a spear in their side. You could see their feet stuck in cement, or chains on their feet. You could see weights on their shoulders.
4. Ask the Lord how He would remove these obstacles. He may have you pull the knife out. You could pray that all the attacks coming against your partner fall to the ground. Perhaps the partner needs to forgive someone for back stabbing him.
5. Ask the Lord to release His spiritual servants to touch your partner, and heal the wounded areas.
6. Switch who is praying and who is receiving.

CHAPTER 3: SEPARATION OF SOUL AND SPIRIT

Let us therefore be diligent to enter that rest, lest anyone fall according to the same example of disobedience. For the word of God is living and powerful, and sharper than any two-edged sword, piercing even to the division of soul and spirit, and of joints and marrow, and is a discerner of the thoughts and intents of the heart.
(Heb. 4:11-12, NKJV)

Who rules?

For those who live according to the flesh set their minds on the things of the flesh, but those who live according to the Spirit, the things of the Spirit. But you are not in the flesh but in the spirit, if indeed the Spirit of God dwells in you. Now if anyone does not have the Spirit of Christ, he is not His. And if Christ is in you, the body is dead because of sin, but the Spirit is life because of righteousness. But if the Spirit of Him who raised Jesus from the dead dwells in you, He who raised Christ from the dead will also give life to your mortal bodies through His Spirit who dwells in you. (Rom. 8:5, 9-11; NKJV)

In the chapter of rest, Hebrews 4, there is a golden nugget, which I believe is a key to entering into the rest and presence of God. Our spirit has been asleep because of sin, but by coming to Christ, it can be awakened. As a result, our spirit still needs to be set free from soul rule. It is the living work of God that does this.

Now he who keeps His commandments abides in Him, and He in him. And by this we know that He abides in us, by the Spirit whom He has given us. (1 John 3:24, NKJV)

WHO'S GOT THE GATES?

Imagine three concentric circles. Next, picture the tabernacle design: the Outer Court (bronze altar), Inner Court, (bronze laver), Holy Place (lampstand, table of showbread, and altar of incense) before the veil leading into the Holy of Holies (Ark of the Covenant) (See page 49). Similarly, our beings consist of the body, soul, and spirit. As explained, the soul has been mediating between the body and spirit, doing what it wants until the spirit is awakened by the Spirit of God.

> *The spirit of a man is the lamp of the Lord, searches; Searching all the innermost parts of his being. (Prov. 20:27, NASB)*

As the spirit of man submits to the Holy Spirit, there is a battle of ruler ship between the spirit, soul, and body. The mind set on the flesh in Romans 8:5 is a description of the soul that is not surrendered to the Holy Spirit and is ruling from a program based on lies, fear, religion, or lust and other deeds of the flesh mentioned in Galatians 5:19-21.

A gateway is a place of authority where dominion is exercised in all its forms. In scripture, gateways were used for business and legal transactions, tax collections, protection, proclamations, and settling disputes (1 Kings 22:10; Ruth 4; Deut. 25:7-9; 2 Sam. 18:24-33). If unrighteousness controls a gate, righteousness will have no access unless we do something to give it a legal right to pass.

The gateways of the spirit, soul, and body may be possessed by the enemies of God blocking our access to the place of rest and abiding as promised in Hebrews 4. In order to enter the place of rest, we need to give the Lord permission to sever the spirit from the soul, and to take possession of the gates of our being surrendering them to the rule and Lordship of Christ Jesus, Holy Spirit, and Father God. By agreeing with the enemy, we have given him legal right to possess the gates of our being. By renouncing these agreements, and taking control of these gates, we can possess them.

Dr. Watchman Nee saw the spirit gates as communion, intuition, and conscience, the soul gates as the mind, will, and emotions, and the body gates as hearing, seeing, smelling, tasting, and touching. By expanding upon this we can include in the spiritual communion gates as prayer, worship, reverence and fear of the Lord. The intuition gate can include revelation, and the conscience gate can include faith and hope. Within the soul gates we can expand the mind gate to include reason, imagination, and the will gate to include choice.

When a person receives the spirit of God, living water carrying the glory of God, flows from the inside out as a spring of love bubbling forth.

> *"But the water that I shall give him will become in him a fountain of water springing up into everlasting life." (John 4:14, NKJ)*

> *"He who believes in Me, as the Scripture has said, out of his heart will flow rivers of living water". But this He spoke concerning the Spirit, whom those believing in Him would receive; for the Holy Spirit was not yet given, because Jesus was not yet glorified. (John 7:38-39, NKJV)*

For a person to connect to the love of God and the presence of God, the gates need to be open. We can open these gates through prayer.

In the following chapter *Cleansing Spirit, Soul, Body Gates* you'll find an example prayer that can be prayed to separate your spirit from the control and dominion of your soul and body and to cleanse the gates so the glory of God can flow through the gates. Focus on the spring of living water within you housing the glory of God. The flow will come from within where the glory of God is and flow through each of the spirit gates, through the soul gates, and through the body gates. It is recommended to pray over each gate individually starting with the spirit gates, flowing through the soul gates, and flowing through the body gates.

> *Now may the God of peace Himself sanctify you completely; and may your whole spirit, soul, and body be preserved blameless at the coming of our Lord Jesus Christ. (1 Thess. 5:23, NKJV)*

CHAPTER 4
CLEANSING SPIRIT, SOUL, BODY GATES

Now may the God of peace Himself sanctify you completely; and may your whole spirit, soul, and body be preserved blameless at the coming of our Lord Jesus Christ.
(1 Thess. 5:23, NKJ)

Father, I surrender to you today. In worship, I offer my body and all parts of my soul as a living sacrifice to You God, holy and pleasing to You. I give You permission to take the sword of the Lord, and separate my spirit from my soul. I invite You Holy Spirit to tabernacle in this body and to fill my innermost being with the glory of God and the love of God and to bubble up and flow from the inside out.

Everywhere I have shut down love and connection to You and others, forgive me. I forgive every person that contributed to my shutting down and building walls, keeping me from love and relationship to You and others. I give you permission to remove the walls constructed by me or others to self-protect but, have left me isolated instead. I break agreements with the walls and the lies of the enemy holding the walls in place.

I hurl down the accusations and the demonic to the feet of Jesus. I command the ungodly guardians of my spirit, soul, and body gates to leave and to go where Jesus would send them. I no longer need their protection. Lord, replace them with your godly beings that will open the gates to good and not to evil. May the glory of God and the love of God fill me and overflow through the spirit gates (communion, intuition, and conscience), the soul gates (mind, will, and emotions), and the body gates (sight, smell, touch, hearing, and taste).

CHAPTER 5
COVENANTS, EXCHANGES, TRADING

For here is the covenant I will one day establish with the people of Israel: I will embed my laws within their thoughts and fasten them onto their hearts. I will be their loyal God and they will be my loyal people.
(Heb. 8:10, TPT)

God has a future and a hope for you. God already has your success, prosperity and fulfillment planned out for you. Your divine birthright that God had for you in the beginning is good. However, often the enemy intercepts the divine birthright by accosting your soul to come into agreement with his plan instead of God's plan at a very young age. Your divine birthright given by God can actually be sabotaged by agreement with the enemy's plan through generational sin, rejection, fear, or through life events when you are a child, in the womb, or even on the way to conception. But thank God that we do not have to remain in that state.

Jesus Christ, our Savior is the mediator of a superior covenant, which supersedes the inferior covenant with the enemy (Heb. 8:6). Jesus is our high priest after the order of Melchizedek (Heb. 7:17). Melchizedek visited Abraham after he had victory over his enemies. In prayer, we renounce agreement with the enemy's plan for our life and ask God to reestablish the divine birthright and destiny He had for us from the beginning. We too will have victory over our enemies as we enter into a blood covenant with our Lord Jesus Christ.

Jesus is the High Priest of the New Covenant. In the new covenant bought by the blood of Jesus, you are His covenant child. Covenant is a solemn and binding commitment between two or more parties. It's a pledge of total loyalty; it goes beyond any other commitment. It's an endless partnership. It cannot be broken under penalty like a contract. Covenant is an absolute commitment; you would lay down your life for your covenant partner. That's the relationship God has always had for you.

He loves you, but because He is holy, your sin separated you from Him. So God made another unconditional blood covenant with you (as He did with Abraham). God allowed His son, His only beloved son, to die for you and be pierced for your sins. You did not do a thing while Jesus poured out His blood and gave up His Spirit for you. He cried, "It is finished!" (John 19:30c, NASB) and "Father, into your hands I commit my Spirit." (Luke 23:46d, NASB). From Matthew 27:51, we learn that the earth shook; there was lightning and thunder. The veil in the temple separating the people from the Holy of Holies was torn from top to bottom. The new covenant is a covenant of faith similar to the Abrahamic covenant of Genesis 15, which God made with Abraham's seed while he slept. In contrast, the Mosaic covenant was conditional, depending upon the obedience of the people to keep the law (Deut. 28). To enter into a covenant with Jesus, you must believe that He paid the price for your sins because He loves you. Economists say that the value of an item is determined by how much someone is willing to pay for it. Our father allowed His son to pay the price for you. Your value to God is the value of His son. He loves you as much as He loves His only begotten son.

THE GREAT EXCHANGE

In covenant, all that He has is yours. All that you have is His.

> *And Jonathan made a covenant with David because he loved him as himself. Jonathan took off the robe he was wearing and gave it to David, along with his tunic, and even his sword, his bow and his belt. (1 Sam 18:3-4, NIV)*

Jesus too, in His incarnation, emptied Himself of a robe of Divinity to put on a robe of humanity to cut a new covenant with His people.

> *He existed in the form of God, yet he gave no thought to seizing equality with God as his supreme prize. Instead he emptied himself of his outward glory by reducing himself to the form of a lowly servant. He became human! (Phil 2:6-7, TPT)*

1. You exchange clothing. Jesus gives His robes of righteousness for your filthy rags. A robe was a symbol of identity. What you wore was a reflection of who you were.

   > *For He has clothed me with the garments of salvation. He has covered me with the robe of righteousness. (Is. 61:10b, NKJV)*

2. You exchange enemies. Your enemies become His and He will contend with you enemies. And now, His enemies are your enemies. Were you wondering why you seemed to have so much coming against you? The enemy hates you!
3. You exchange weapons. He gives you spiritual weapons for your fleshly weapons.

AGREEMENTS AND TRADES

Often when praying for someone, desiring freedom, I ask the Lord, what is the legal right for the accuser of the brethren to come against this one? The answers are various. The answers could be sin committed by the individual or generational sin, covenants or agreements made with the enemy, or trauma from abuse. The enemy comes to steal, kill, and destroy (John 10:10). As a believer, once you have received the Lord Jesus Christ, and accepted his death as payment for your sins, you are making a trade with heaven, and set free. In the divine exchange of making a blood covenant with Father God through the blood of Jesus, there is an exchange. In covenant, there is an exchange of robes, weapons, and enemies. However, by making agreements with the enemy, believing lies, or committing sin, you are making trades with the kingdom of darkness. When you trade with the enemy, in thought, word, or deed, knowingly or unknowingly, you give the enemy legal right to come against you. By ungodly trading, you could be pulled out from under the protective hand of Father God.

> *Like a flitting sparrow, like a flying swallow, so a curse without cause shall not alight. (Prov. 26:2, NKJV)*

We can trade with the Kingdom of light, or with the kingdom of darkness. A trade is an exchange. Our thoughts and actions can be a trading platform. What you think about is a trade for who you become. What you focus on, you empower. In trading, you reap what you sow. If you sow strawberry seeds, you'll get strawberries. We can sow by our words, speaking words of life or words of death. When God spoke, He created, and likewise, by your words and thoughts, you can create. If you are fearful of getting sick, your very thoughts and words of worry can bring on you the condition you are focused on.

> *"You were the anointed cherub who covers, and I placed you there. You were on the holy mountain of God; you walked in the midst of the stones of fire. "You were blameless in your ways from the day you were created until unrighteousness was found in you. "By the abundance of your trade you were internally filled with violence, and you sinned; therefore I have cast you as profane from the mountain of God. And I have destroyed you, O covering cherub, from the midst of the stones of fire. "Your heart was lifted up because of your beauty; you corrupted your wisdom by reason of your splendor. I cast you to the ground; I put you before kings, that they may see you. (Ezek. 28:14-17, NASB)*

> *How you have fallen from heaven, O star of the morning, son of the dawn! You have been cut down to the earth, you who have weakened the nations! But you said in your heart, I will ascend to heaven; I will raise my throne above the stars of God, and I will sit on the mount of assembly in the recesses of the north. I will ascend above the heights of the clouds; I will make myself like the Most High. Nevertheless, you will be thrust down to Sheol, to the recesses of the pit. (Isa. 14: 12-15, NASB)*

In Ezekiel 28, Satan traded his position of being a covering cherub, so he could be like God. Lucifer, a covering cherub of God's glory, traded the revelation he got from God for himself so he could be exalted. It was a trade of pride, and worship of self. It was the same trade he presented to Eve to eat of the tree of the knowledge of good and evil. He deceived a third of the angels who fell with him, mankind in the garden, and attempted to deceive our Lord Jesus who would not trade with him. He had access to all knowledge, yet in self-exaltation, he was cast down. What you do in the natural has effect in the spirit realm, and what you do in the spirit realm affects the natural realm.

When mankind fell, by trading on Satan's trading floor, they relinquished and lost the dominion rule over creation that they had been given. When we trade with the kingdom of darkness, there is a cost and a loss. We can lose our purpose, our crowns, our treasures and blessings God has for us. But, Jesus came. When Jesus came, He refused to trade His God given purpose for reconciling mankind to God, for His own personal rule of the kingdoms Satan had stolen from man.

> *Again, the devil took Him to a very high mountain and showed Him all the kingdoms of the world and their glory; and he said to Him, "All these things will I give You, if You fall down and worship me." Then Jesus said to him, "Go Satan! For it is written, 'You shall worship the Lord Your God, and serve Him only.'" (Matt. 4:8-10, NASB)*

The enemy is a roaring lion seek to devour with the purpose to kill, steal, and destroy (1 Pet. 5:8; John 10:10). When you trade with the enemy, there is a cost and a loss. The ungodly trade opens a door to the enemy and gives him legal right to steal, kill, and destroy. In your life and generational line, there has been loss of identity, loss of purpose, loss of gifts, loss of dominion, loss of blessings, loss of finances, loss of health, loss of hope, loss of joy, loss of motivation, and the list goes on. Satan's authority to rule the earth was given to him by deception and trade with Adam and Eve. But, Jesus got the authority and the keys back, by His death so man could be reconciled to God, and our purpose to rule is restored (Rev. 1:18). By entering into a blood covenant with Jesus, a godly trade, we can retain the losses and rule. In fact, scripture says we can get a seven-fold restoration. Hallelujah!

> *And Jesus came up and spoke to them, saying, "All authority has been given to Me in heaven and earth. Go therefore and make disciples of all the nations, baptizing them in the name of the Father and the Son and the Holy Spirit." (Matt. 28: 18-19, NASB)*

CHAPTER 6: SIN AND GENERATIONAL CURSES

"You shall not worship them or serve them; for I, the Lord your God, am a jealous God, visiting the iniquity of the fathers on the children, on the third and fourth generations of those who hate me, but showing loving-kindness to thousands, to those who love me and keep my commandments."
(Ex. 20:5, NASB)

What are some of the ungodly trades we make with the enemy that give the enemy legal right to steal, kill, and destroy? Legal right can be given through our own personal sin, generational sin, or making covenants with evil.

> *Then I acknowledged my sin to you and did not cover up my iniquity. I said, "I will confess my transgressions to the Lord." And you forgave the guilt of my sin. (Ps. 32:5, NIV)*

Sin means to miss the mark, as in archery. It can mean doing something against God or a person, (Ex. 10:16), and doing the opposite of what is right (Gal. 5:17). Transgression refers to presumptuous sin. It means to choose to intentionally disobey, willful trespassing. When we knowingly run a stop sign, tell a lie, or blatantly disregard an authority, this is transgressing. Iniquity is linked to generational sin.

> *Blessed is the one whose transgressions are forgiven, whose sins are covered. (Ps. 32:1, NIV)*

> *Iniquity is deeply rooted and means premeditated choice, continuing to sin without repentance. "Woe to those who plan iniquity, to those who plot evil on their beds!" (Mic. 2:1, NIV)*

There has been ungodly trading by your ancestors that give the accuser legal right to steal from you. By identificational repentance and renouncing what your family line or nation has done, you can remove the curse. By stepping into your call as a priest, you can forgive, and wash with the blood of Jesus. Whom you forgive God forgives. You are bringing reconciliation of yourself, your generational line, and your nation to God.

Generational curses result when our ancestors knowingly or unknowing trade with the enemy. We see people with addictions in their family line being passed on to the next generations (Deut. 28). A grandfather may be an alcoholic, but the grandson becomes addicted to drugs. A father may have an affair at age 30, and at the same age, his son is tempted to have an affair. Kris Vallotton talks about struggling with thoughts of death and finds out his father did too. A witchcraft curse came on the family when his mother had her future read by tarot cards. Chuck Piece talks about his family's financial struggle until the curse of poverty was broken. Unless these strongholds are broken, the enemy has legal right to come against you and your children.

Our ancestors have even traded their future generation's inheritance and blessing for their own immediate gratification. An example of this is our nation's skyrocketing debt going into trillions since 1980. The previous generation spent, so the next generations have to pay and will always be in debt. What is true in the natural is true in the spiritual. Another example is freemasonry. Dedications of families to the great architect resulted in horrible, disgusting curses to be brought on families. My own grandfather was a 33rd degree mason, so I was the one to break the curses off my family.

Generationally, our ancestors have traded on some ungodly trading floors. Some ungodly trading floors are mentioned in the next chapter, and some are mentioned in The Prayer to Establish God's New Foundation, in Chapter 13. Unless we have renounced the ungodly trading, agreements, and covenants our ancestors have made, we are still under the curse, and the enemy has legal right to come against us. Let me be clear, I do not spend my time looking for devils. I've been there and done that having been a deliverance minister for 13 years. My purpose is to lead people into freedom and fullness so they can be all that God has called them to be. The Lord has revealed better, and more efficient ways to walk in the fullness and abundance God has for us. Renunciation and breaking agreements with the ungodly covenants is a key to setting people free so they can be overcomers, established in Him.

CHAPTER 7 TRADING FLOORS

"By the abundance of your trade, you were internally filled with violence, and you sinned; therefore, I have cast you as profane from the mountain of God. And I have destroyed you, O covering cherub, from the midst of the stones of fire."
(Ezek. 28:16, NASB)

If you choose to love sin, it will become your master, and it will own you and reward you with death. But if you choose to love and obey God, he will lead you into perfect righteousness.
(Rom. 6:16B, TPT)

As mentioned in chapter 5, our thoughts and actions can be trading platforms. What you think about is a trade for who you become. This is why what we think upon is so powerful, because we create by our thoughts, words, and actions. In everything we do, we either trade with the kingdom of light, or with the kingdom of darkness. Our trades can open or close the door to the enemy. By allowing our thoughts to dwell upon the negative, and criticism, we open a door for the enemy to come in. By repenting, renouncing, and forgiving our family lines and ourselves for partnering with the ungodly spirits, and trading on their trading floor, we can be set free. What are some of the ungodly trading floors that we and our generational line have traded upon that we need to break agreement with?

SOME UNGODLY TRADING FLOORS

1. **Python; Witchcraft (Deut. 18:10; 2 Kings 17:17; 2 Kings 21:6).**

    a. Divination, Sorcery, Pharmekia (mind altering drugs). Turning to drugs, oral.

    b. Rebellion – Against God; as the sin of witchcraft (1 Sam. 15:23).

        i. Wanting to do things one's own way, instead of God's way.

c. Restricts and chokes the life, wind, and breathe from a person to put him in bondage and thwart his purpose. Kills prayer lives.

   d. Attempts to take out people who are pressing into God.

   e. False prophetic spirit, attempts to distract and derail the true prophetic; persecutes a move of God

2. **Baal (1 Kings 18: 18-40, Judg. 6:25-32)**

   a. Babylonian deity - The thunder god; god of sky, rain, fertility

   b. Worship included human sacrifice and sexual immorality

   c. Self-mutilation

3. **Queen of Heaven (Jer. 44:17-25)**

   a. Counterfeit Holy Spirit

   b. Under this principality are goddesses of various names dependent upon the region such as Greek, Roman or Caananite. For example, Istar, Diana, and Asherah are goddesses and demons of lust and fertility. Athena and Minerva (on the California seal) are goddesses and demons of the sea, trade, war and wisdom.

4. **Jezebel (1 Kings 16:31; 1 Kings 18:4 & 19:2; 1 Kings 21:5-25; 2 Kings 9:7-37; Rev. 2:20)**

   This spirit also partners with the Queen of Heaven. When the Jezebel spirit attacks church leadership, its ultimate purpose will be to disable the spiritual authority of pastoral leadership. The attack may come in the form of sexual temptation, confusion or prophetic manipulation, but its aim is to supplant the authority in the church. The Jezebel spirit seeks to divide, diminish, and then displace the spiritual authority God has given church leaders. Because the spirit is against authority in the church, it will seek to put wedges of division between a pastor and the church intercessors.

   a. Control, manipulation, intimidation; Baal worship

   b. Envy, jealousy, gossip, confusion

   c. False prophet, seeks to destroy the true prophetic

   d. Attacks church leadership to disable spiritual authority

   e. Attacks could be in the form of sexual temptation or seduction

5. **Ahab (1 Kings 16:28-33; 1 Kings 18:1 & 19:1; 1 Kings 21:1-29)**

   a. Passive aggressive, controlled, stirred up by Jezebel

    b. Stole the vineyard of Naboth, a righteous man, and kills him following Jezebel's orders

    c. Hides in cave

    d. Partners with Jezebel

6. **Leviathan (Job 41:1, Ps. 74:14 & 104:26, Isa. 27:1)**

    a. Gate keeper of mind control; unseen battle over your mind

    b. Twisting serpent twists your words, and the words spoken to you (Ps. 56:5)

    c. Perverter of truth

    d. Divides key relationships in families, churches, work

    e. Accuses you, and causes you to accuse others.

    f. Seven heads which are: pride, a critical spirit, confusion, impatience, deception, contention, and discord.

7. **Cain (Gen. 4:6-16)**

    a. Kills one's brother (i.e. the previous move of God judges and attempts to kill the next move of God).

    b. It's possible to commit murder in your heart by holding onto hatred (Matt. 5:27-28).

8. **Tyre, Spirit of Mammon (Ezek. 28: 1-5)**

    a. Spirit of greed and not having enough

    b. Demon takes finances from the church. King Tyre took money from the temple treasuries to build a trading port that robbed from people.

    c. Poverty Spirit; spirit of lack

        i. Meager possibilities

    d. Orphan Spirit

        i. Fatherlessness - Not having identity as a son.

9. **Fear**

    a. Fear of man, man pleaser, anxiety,

10. Free Masonry

Secret society for men who worship the great architect of the universe. and the symbol is the all seeing eye which represents the Egyptian god Osiris. Rituals and vows made during ceremonies and rites bring curses to the family lines. Leviathan partners with this spirit.

11. Korah Spirit (Num. 16)

A leader who wants it all. Able to seduce 250 of Israel's princes to join him in a rebellion against Moses. Korah claims that Moses is rebelling against God and is domineering in his leadership. It is Korah who is seeking to exalt himself, yet he accuses Moses and Aaron of exalting themselves above the assembly. Our wrong attitude toward authority will cause us to misjudge a leader as controlling when he is in fact simply fulfilling his God given spiritual responsibility. Moses exposes the sin of envy and ambition in Korah's heart. Ambition has two parts, envy and pride. Whenever we covet the position that God has assigned to another, we are attracting the Lord's anger to ourselves.

12. Absalom Spirit (2 Sam. 15)

Prince Absalom sought the throne of King David and stole the hearts of the people. He encouraged grumbling in the people of Israel while winning the hearts of the people with flattery and charm. These are the ones who cause divisions. The plan of the Absalom spirit is simple, grumble about the way things are not getting done, find fault with the leader, and arrogantly project the image that if you were in charge all would be well. The spirit seeks to capture the hearts of the people, flatter them and bring them into their camp.

13. Religious Spirit (Matt. 22:15-22)

A spirit using religious structures to entangle people in bondage, prevent transformation, and keep the status quo. It comes against the anointing, revelation, prophetic insight, and uses tradition to build structures of limitation. Through criticism, complaints, fear of man, fiery passion turns to lukewarm.

The antidote for these influences is true humility, breaking agreement with the spirit, and not partnering with it.

CHAPTER 8: TREASURES OF DARKNESS PROPHETIC WORD

*"And I will give you the treasures of darkness and hidden wealth of
secret places, so that you may know that it is I, the Lord, the God of Israel,
who calls you by your name."*
(Isa. 45:3, NASB)

Ungodly trading at the gates;
Commodities;
My people left behind their first love, their passion for me;
They lost their light, and traded with my foe;
Adam and Eve traded all I gave them with the enemy;
They lost not only for themselves but for future generations the glory.

This is a time and season to take back what was lost, stolen, and given away;
I want my bride to return to me;
I call you home;
I gave all to buy you back;
My death and blood and sacrifice was to buy you back;
So you might be free, and return to me;

And I return to you what I gave you originally;
Glory in the garden;
Fellowship with Me in the garden;
Joy, hope, and everlasting life with Me.

Adam traded his glory for a fig leaf;
Jacob's brother gave up his birthright for a meal.
Lost, lost are the treasures of darkness;
Legal right was given in disobedience;
The scales are imbalanced;
The sins of Babylon are to be judged;
Restoration of the flesh is coming.

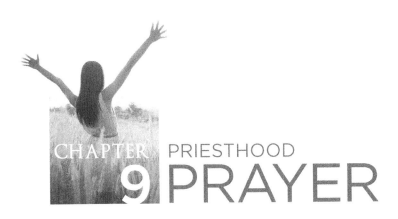

CHAPTER 9 — PRIESTHOOD PRAYER

You also, as living stones, are being built up as a spiritual house for a holy priesthood, to offer up spiritual sacrifices acceptable to God through Jesus Christ.

But you are A CHOSEN RACE, A royal PRIESTHOOD, A HOLY NATION, A PEOPLE FOR GOD'S OWN POSSESSION, that you may proclaim the excellencies of Him who has called you out of darkness into His marvelous light; for you once were NOT A PEOPLE but now you are THE PEOPLE OF GOD; you had NOT RECEIVED MERCY, but now you have RECEIVED MERCY.
(1 Pet. 2:5, 9-10; NASB)

When I speak of breaking the curses, I am not talking about focusing on the devil, contending with him and fighting on ground level. I am talking about putting on the priestly robes and authority as a priest, stepping into the presence of God, and presenting the case before the throne. As a priest would wash himself first in the bronze laver, in the Outer Courts, so we wash ourselves in the blood of Jesus. As a priest offers a sacrifice on the bronze altar in the Inner Court, we offer ourselves as a living sacrifice to the Lord, a godly trade on the altar of Jesus, identifying with His death for us. As a priest steps into the Holy Place, we eat of the bread of life in communion of Jesus, at the table of showbread, being filled with the oil, light and spirit of the Lord at the lamp stand, and offer the prayers of the saints on the altar of incense. We are even able to step through the veil and have direct access to God, receiving mercy at the mercy seat of God. (See page 49)

> *As obedient children, do not be conformed to the former lusts which were yours in your ignorance, but like the Holy One who called you, be holy yourselves also in all your behavior; because it is written, "YOU SHALL BE HOLY, FOR I AM HOLY." (1 Pet. 1:14-15, NASB)*

We don't walk in the authority Jesus has given us. We have let the enemy steal our identity, and purpose. We don't know that we are called to put on the holy garments of the priest, and to forgive the sins of our people. It is written, we shall be holy as He is holy. Jesus said we would do greater things than He did. How? By believing, and reconciling our people and creation back to him.

Romans 8:14-22 states that the whole earth eagerly waits for the revelation of the Sons of God. Creation, subjected to futility and corruption because of man's sin, groans for the children of God to take their place and dominion as Sons of God. We too groan within for the day of redemption and restoration. I believe that we have entered into the time of Reconciliation and Restoration. God is revealing His sons, those who know Him in a unique way this season so they can reign and bring restoration to the Kingdom.

How is this happening you ask? It is through receiving the Light of God, connecting to the Light, ascending into heavenly places, reconciling and restoring what has been lost, stolen, and given away. It is the time of reconciliation and restoration of all things.

> *Then he showed me Joshua the high priest standing before the Angel of the Lord, and Satan standing at his right hand to oppose him. And the Lord said to Satan, "The Lord rebuke you, Satan! The Lord who has chosen Jerusalem rebuke you! Is this not a brand plucked from the fire?" Now Joshua was clothed with filthy garments, and was standing before the Angel. Then He answered and spoke to those who stood before Him, saying, "Take away the filthy garments from him." And to him He said, "See I have removed your iniquity from you, and I will clothe you with rich robes." And I said, "Let them put a clean turban on his head." So they put a clean turban on his head, and they put the clothes on him.*
>
> *And the Angel of the Lord stood by. Then the Angel of the Lord admonished Joshua, saying, "Thus says the Lord of hosts: 'If you will walk in My ways, and if you will keep My command, then you shall also judge My house, and likewise have charge of My courts; I will give you places to walk among those who stand here.' (Zech. 3:1-7, NASB)*

Courtroom prayer is scriptural. As priests, we are invited to walk in His ways, keep His commands, judge His house and take charge of His courts. In the courtrooms of heavens, decisions are made, that will manifest upon the earth. This is where the battle is fought efficiently and effectively. Otherwise we are wasting our time binding and casting out devils.

The spirit realm works by laws that govern the spiritual realm. The accuser of the brethren as well as demonic entities are allowed to go into certain courtrooms to present their legal rights to the judge to get permission to come against you. (2 Chron. 18:18-21; Job 1:6-7; Job 2:1-4; Luke 22:31-34). As priests, when we go to the courtrooms, for ourselves or for those we are representing, the accusers have to show up. We can request that they be bound and gagged. I often notice when I hit the target in prayer by the reaction of the accusers. We present our case, repenting, renouncing, and forgiving sin, covering it with the blood. We strip the enemy of the legal right to come against us by repentance, renouncing and by the washing of the blood of the lamb.

> *And they overcame him by the blood of the Lamb and by the word of their testimony, and they did not love their lives to the death. (Rev. 12:11, NKJV)*

After we have repented and renounce the ungodly trades, we ask the Lord for the legal papers to evict the enemy from our lives, families, and spheres of influence. We send the demonic to Jesus to deal with. We receive the papers and partner with God in judging the enemy. We take the legal papers and trade on the blood and body of Jesus for redemption and restoration.

Since 2006, God has been giving me revelation piece by piece about the ungodly grid, and the godly grid. In a dream in 2006, God told me to go into the ungodly dimensional grid to retrieve those stuck, but I had to be a minor. I woke up and wondered how I could go back in time to become a minor, younger than 21, but God later revealed I was to be a miner, one that searches for and uncovers the gold in people. The ungodly grid is an ungodly trading floor. I would see people stuck in nets, under sewage grates, in jail, behind cages and fences. They were stuck because of ungodly trading. In 2009, in Australia, the Lord showed me the handwriting on the wall. First I saw the quadrants, then the number 64, and then a chessboard. The freemasons in ritual traded their generations on a chessboard. Ancestors have traded with ungodly spiritual beings, demons, kings, or principalities, by coming into agreement with the enemy allowing him access to steal elements, building blocks, and treasures to build his kingdom. Through prayer, and breaking ungodly covenants, contracts and agreement with the enemy, one is able to be set free from building one's life on the ungodly foundation, and be released to build on the godly foundation of the Lord.

In 2009, I wrote the Treasures of Darkness prayer, and 2010, the Lord gave me the Foundation prayer to disconnect people from the ungodly foundations generationally in order to connect to the godly foundation. This is when the Lord gave me the revelation of the godly trading floor.

Satan is a counterfeit of the righteous real. Just as there have been ungodly altars and trading floors, such as in freemasonry, there is also a godly trading floor in heaven. In Genesis 1 God speaks of the firmament.

> *Then God said, "Let there be a firmament in the midst of the waters, and let it divide the waters from the waters." (Gen. 1:6, NKJV)*

> *Thus God made the firmament, and divided the waters which were under the firmament from the waters which were above the firmament; and it was so. (Gen 1:7, NKJV)*

And God called the firmament Heaven. So the evening and the morning were the second day. (Gen 1:8, NKJV)

Then God said, "Let there be lights in the firmament of the heavens to divide the day from the night; and let them be for signs and seasons, and for days and years; (Gen 1:14, NKJV)

And let them be for lights in the firmament of the heavens to give light on the earth"; and it was so. (Gen 1:15, NKJV)

God set them in the firmament of the heavens to give light on the earth. (Gen 1:17, NKJV)

Later, I find that the same Hebrew word for firmament is the Crystal Sea mentioned in Ezekiel and Revelation.

The likeness of the firmament above the heads of the living creatures was like the color of an awesome crystal, stretched out over their heads. (Ezek. 1:22, NKJV)

And under the firmament their wings spread out straight, one toward another. Each one had two, which covered one side, and each one had two, which covered the other side of the body. (Ezek. 1:23, NKJV)

A voice came from above the firmament that was over their heads; whenever they stood, they let down their wings. (Ezek. 1:25, NKJV)

And above the firmament over their heads was the likeness of a throne, in appearance like a sapphire stone; on the likeness of the throne was a likeness with the appearance of a man high above it. (Ezek. 1:26, NKJV)

And I looked, and there in the firmament that was above the head of the cherubim, there appeared something like a sapphire stone, having the appearance of the likeness of a throne. (Ezek. 10:1, NKJV)

And before the throne there was something like a sea of glass, like crystal; and in the center and around the throne, four living creatures full of eyes in front and behind. (Rev. 4:6, NASB)

The Crystal Sea, where the throne of God is established, is the righteous trading floor. The 24 elders cast their crowns before the throne in worship and trade before the Lord worthy to receive glory, honor, and power. The Crystal Sea is the Firmament, holding heavenly lights, the Foundation of the throne of God and connected to the New Foundation upon which the Lord is building, the New Jerusalem. I was amazed to find out that Crystalline structures of gemstones are cubes, lattices, and grids. I became convinced that the Crystal Sea is the godly trading floor where we are to take our papers, and even our crowns and trade to get the restoration of all things back to God.

Jesus is a priest forever according to the order of Melchizedek (Heb. 5:6). Hebrews 7 continues that Melchizedek, king of Salem (Peace), priest of the Most High God meets Abraham after his victory and blesses him. We note that Abraham gave a tithe to this king of righteousness and king of peace, without father, mother or genealogy, having neither beginning of days or end of life. After victory over the enemy, we too trade on the blood and body of Jesus. We take our courtroom papers, and do the divine exchange on God's foundation of righteousness and justice. We exchange relationship with God for separation, liberty for the captives, comfort for mourning, beauty for ashes, the oil of joy for mourning, the garment of praise for the spirit of heaviness, and double honor for shame (Isa. 61).

In summary, spiritual discernment is essential for mature believers, so we are not deceived by every wind of doctrine, speculation and deceit coming our way. To discern properly and allow the spirit from within to flow out, it is important to separate the soul from the spirit, and cleanse the gates, the spirit gates, the soul gates, and the body gates. Priestly Heavenly Courtroom prayer can be a valuable tool to renounce the strongholds in our personal lives and generationally so we can be free to step into the purposes God has for us. In this process, "ungodly trading" and "godly trading" were introduced. What we think, speak, and act upon, we create in our lives. The seeds we sow reap a harvest, good or evil. We can exchange the old for the new to receive the fullness God has for us. These tools empower us to no longer live in meagerness, but in abundance.

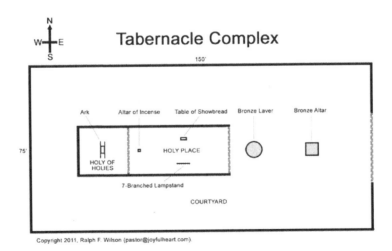

CHAPTER 10
HEAVENLY COURTROOM PRAYER PROTOCOL

Thus says the Lord of hosts: 'If you will walk in My ways, and if you will keep My command, then you shall also judge My house, and likewise have charge of My courts; I will give you places to walk among those who stand here.
(Zech. 3:7, NASB)

1. **Rest** – Abide in Him. Step into the presence (into the spirit) resting in him. "I thank you, you are here."

2. **Rapture** – As you step into His presence in the blood, you are being washed. You don't have to be so concerned what you are bringing in, you are being rinsed off.

3. **Re-garment** – Put on the rich robes of Christ's righteousness (Zech. 3).

4. **Rinsed** – As you go up with him, the anxiety and things that would hold you back fly off. Give him all your concerns and allow Him to clean you. It's the Shepherd's job to clean the sheep. As you are in his presence don't be concerned that you don't pray it just right. Present yourself as a living sacrifice before the Lord.

5. **Request** – Take me to the Court Room you have for me today. There are different Court Rooms that function differently. You may see a gavel, lot of light, judge (father God). Everyone will see slightly differently.

6. **Records and Rights of the Accuser** – Ask the Lord, to reveal the legal Rights and Records of the enemy to come against you and your family line. These are records of sin you and your family line has committed.

7. **Round up** – Ask for the Lord to bring the accusers into the Courtroom bound and gagged, so they cannot accuse or condemn you. Lord, please gag them and bind the spirits.

8. **Repent** – Repent, Renounce, and Forgive of sins on behalf of yourself and your generational line and for trading on the enemy's trading floor. Break agreements with the enemy. When the enemy tells you a lie and you believe, you just traded on the enemy's trading floor. As a Priest, you forgive and wash with the blood of Jesus. Whom you forgive (including yourself), God forgives.

9. **Request Papers** – Request the divorce papers for you personally. For a region, ask for eviction notices. Wait for the divorce papers to come; sometimes it's a huge stack. On the papers, the Father God has to go through every paper that is presented to him. You can pray about something else while it is being processed. Usually you may notice they're signed "Paid by the Blood" or sealed with a signet ring.

10. **Receive the papers. Thank the Lord.**

11. **Rule** – Judge the evil; either you or the Lord bangs the gavel. (I judge the evil in the name of Jesus. You want them away and you don't want them to come back.)

12. **Remove** – Send all the demonic to the feet of Jesus to deal with.

13. **Replace** – The godly trade is done upon the body and blood of Jesus and upon God's foundation, the Crystal Sea.

    a. For example, trade fear for love, courage or peace, but most importantly trade for intimacy with Jesus. You can exchange for the fruit of spirit, and the 7 spirits of God.

    b. Melchizedek is the keeper of the Resources God has for you.

14. **Receive the Resources** – You need to put in a safe place such your belly. The Lord may show you a safe place. The Lord may show you a safe place

15. **Release** – Release the declarations, in heaven and on earth. Releasing is making the declarations. Declare what you want (i.e. in a job). Declarations are more powerful when done in heaven.

16. **Restore** – Restore the earth, rebuild. Bring God's kingdom to earth.

CHAPTER 11: DIVINE EXCHANGE

And provide for those who grieve in Zion—to bestow on them a crown of beauty instead of ashes, the oil of joy instead of mourning, and a garment of praise instead of a spirit of despair. They will be called oaks of righteousness, a planting of the Lord for the display of his splendor.
(Isa. 61:3, NIV)

Divine Exchange – We exchange the old for the new. Re-garment by taking off the old and putting on the new. As you recall in the Courtroom Prayer, we always exchange the old for the new that God has for us.

WHAT WE TAKE OFF

Masks, clothes to disguise
(1 Sam. 28:8)

Heavy yokes
(1 Kings 12:4,9; 2 Chron. 10:4,9)

Garments of mourning
(Est. 4:1; 2 Sam. 14:2; Jonah 3:5)

Shame
(Isa. 61)

WHAT WE PUT ON

His Righteousness
(Job 29:14; Isa. 59:17; Eph. 4:24)
Breastplate of Righteousness
(Eph. 6:14)

His yoke
(Matt. 11:29, 30)

Royal robes
(1 Kings 22:30)

Priestly Garments
(Lev. 6:10)

WHAT WE TAKE OFF	WHAT WE PUT ON
Garments of widowhood (Gen. 38:19)	**His Love** (Col. 3:14); **Love incorruptible** (Eph. 6:24)
Lay aside the deeds of darkness (Rom. 13:12)	**His armor of light** (Rom. 13:12)
Human wisdom (1 Cor. 2:5)	**The mind of Christ** (1 Cor. 2:16); **God's wisdom** (1 Cor. 2:6-7)
Garments of mourning, ashes, depression (Isa. 61:3)	**Crown of beauty, mantle of praise, oil of gladness, thanksgiving** (Is 61:2-3 NKJV)
	Armor of God (Jer. 46:4, Eph. 6:11-17)

CHAPTER 12: PRAYER TO BECOME A LIVING SACRIFICE

Therefore I urge you, brethren, by the mercies of God, to present your bodies a living and holy sacrifice, acceptable to God, which is your spiritual service of worship.
(Rom. 12:1, NASB)

Thank You, Father God, for making a way for us to come boldly into Your Presence. By faith we walk through the torn Veil into the Holy of Holies and with total abandonment, we now lay ourselves on the altar to You, Lord Jesus, our High Priest. Lord Jesus, today we yield our lives in a fresh way to You. We surrender our lives and testimony of the record that is within each one of us that is held in our blood, for life is in the blood.

Lord Jesus, as our High Priest, we invite You to take Your Word like a sword and circumcise our hearts, taking out all of the hidden secret things and bringing total purity and holiness back into all the hidden secret things of the testimony of each one of our lives: things we have done, things that we have pretended, things we have walked in, things we have said, things we have participated with, and things that have been done to us.

Lord, remove the false coverings, all pretenses, masks, and the defense and coping mechanisms that we have placed upon our lives to get the approval of others and even of You, Father God. Remove every old fig leaf!

We bow our heads in surrender to Your government and come away from where we have aligned our thinking with worldly mindsets, drawing our reasoning from the tree of the knowledge of good and evil. We give you permission to remove trauma and negative emotions from our innermost being, and to cleanse our immune system and our spine where the fear of man has kept chaos locked in our bodies and souls.

Replace the fear of man with the Fear of the Lord. Take out our stony hearts, and replace with a pure and tender heart full of faith and hope to see the unseen things and a heart full of light with limitless capacity to grow in the Love of God. May our heart beat with your heart, Lord Jesus. Renew our minds in Christ, and give us revelation knowledge and eyes to see what you Father God are doing so we can partner with you.

CHAPTER 13
PRAYER TO ESTABLISH GOD'S NEW FOUNDATION

Righteousness and justice are the foundation of Your throne;
Lovingkindness and truth go before You.
(Ps. 89:14, NASB)

By Dale Shannon
12/6/10

Lord, I ask You to build Your godly structure in my life, family, and ministry built upon love, faith and hope, and to tear down ungodly structures built on selfishness, pride, and selfish ambition.

Lord, I repent and renounce for myself and my ancestors for building ungodly structures based on man's agenda, pride, honor, fame, self-centeredness, greed, rebellion, and worship of self instead of worshiping the One True God.[1]

Lord, I repent and renounce for myself and my ancestors for not receiving the words of God, desiring to know You, Father God, and building upon the rock of God, but instead, building upon the foolishness of man and the sand which does not stand.[2]

I repent for myself and my ancestors for not receiving Jesus as the Christ, the Son of the Living God enabling us to build a righteous structure that would prevail against the attacks of hell and the winds of destruction.

Lord, I repent for myself and my ancestors for rejecting You, Lord Jesus, the chief cornerstone, precious, and chosen by God, and allowing You to become a stumbling block and rock of offense.[3,4]

---

[1] Gen. 11 The Tower of Babel
[2] Matt. 7:21-27 Building upon the Rock

Lord, bring the Living Stones into alignment with You, the chief cornerstone, Lord Jesus. Align me to Your sound and Your frequency, that I may vibrate and resonate with You Lord Jesus.

Lord, remove all ungodly grids from my mind and brain causing division and double mindedness. Remove all that has shut down connections between the right and left side of my brain. Release my mind and brain from ungodly dimensional places, heights and depths. Take away double mindedness and all that would keep me from worshiping You single mindedly.

Lord, remove all ungodly grids from my heart and soul causing division. Remove anything from the heart chambers, and quadrants that would keep life from flowing in and out of the quadrants freely. Release my heart and emotions from all ungodly dimensional places, heights and depths, and remove all division of my heart, that I may love you wholeheartedly with single focus.

Lord, I repent and renounce for myself and my ancestors for losing our first love for You, and allowing the lampstands to be taken to build the enemy's kingdom. Lord, restore first love, and release the stolen lampstands taken from individuals, families, ministries, and churches. Lord shine Your light again.[5,6]

I repent for myself and my ancestors for building on self-effort, might, and power instead of building on the Spirit of God. I ask You Lord to remove the mountains of resistance to building Your foundation, and I ask that the capstone be laid through Your grace and mercy. Lord, I declare that You are my Refuge and Strength. Lord, build Your houses of refuge and safety for Your people.

Lord, release the cleansing whirlwind of Your Holy Spirit to cleanse the contamination off the elements of my being and my DNA and RNA, and restore all that is missing. I ask that my temple be aligned to the plumb line of Your Holy Temple and that my DNA and RNA be cleansed by the blood of Jesus and joined to the DNA / RNA of the Trinity: Father, Son, and Holy Spirit.[7] Integrate my DNA / RNA with the Trinity and into the godly Living Stone that You have ordained for me. As a Living Stone, I desire to build Your Spiritual House, and to be part of Your holy priesthood offering spiritual sacrifices acceptable to You through Christ Jesus.[8]

Lord, I repent and renounce for myself and my ancestors for building an ungodly trading floor, an ungodly grid, and trading the future generation's benefits for instant gratification.

---

[3] Matt. 16:16 -19 Peter's confession
[4] 1 Pet. 2:6-7
[5] Rev. 2:4-5
[6] Faulty Foundation dream, 10/22/10
[7] Zech. 4:7-10
[8] 1 Pet. 2:4-7

PRAYER TO ESTABLISH GOD'S NEW FOUNDATION

On behalf of my ancestors and myself, I repent and renounce for engaging in trade with a network of ungodly deities from Babylon, Egypt, and the Philistines. I break all oaths, covenants and agreements made with ungodly principalities, spirit kings, and thrones such as Queen of Heaven, Baal, Ra, Artemis, Nimrod, Babylon, Tyre[9], Jezebel[10], Athelia[11], Delilah[12], Apollyon[13], Leviathan[14], and Cain[15]. Lord would you topple the ungodly thrones, and exchange the ungodly trading floor with Your godly trading floor? Lord I ask for a seven-fold return of what has been lost, stolen, and given away in my generational line. I pray for the New Jerusalem to be built on foundations of righteousness and justice.

Lord, remove all ungodly grids, foundations, and thrones built on the ungodly foundations causing disunity and separation from You. Lord, break all ungodly connections between me and ungodly thrones, grids, networks, guardians, dimensional places, beings, demons, entities, tormentors and voices, and remove all traps, snares, and lassos that would try to reconnect me. I break and renounce all covenants and agreements that my ancestors and I made with ungodly world dominions, rulers, systems, and beliefs, and I ask you to disconnect me from them.

Lord, connect me to Your godly firmament, expanse, foundation of Your throne, the Crystal Sea. Release your white stone bringing clarity in perception and prayer for the nations. Release Your light connecting me to You and Your light source. Rightly align the body of Christ together in unity, connecting the Living Stones, the cubes, with righteousness and justice building Your New Foundation, the New Jerusalem.

Lord, release the whirlwind of Your Spirit, and Your horses to prepare for the building of the godly foundation, the New Jerusalem. Lord, connect me to Your righteous foundation, Your godly firmament, the crystal sea, Your throne, and Your godly network.

Lord release the gifts of the spirit to equip me and connect me to You and the body of Christ in unity of faith, maturity, fullness of Christ, joined and knit together, each doing our share, edifying one another in love. Lord, may each of Your Living Stones shine with Your light, glory, uniqueness, creativity, and be released in the flow of Your symphonic harmony, radiating Your light, wisdom, joy, peace and love to a lost and dying world.

---

[9] Tyre: spirit of greed and not having enough
[10] Jezebel: spirit of control
[11] Athelia: spirit of failure, worthlessness
[12] Delilah: spirit of seduction
[13] Apollyon: spirit of fear of witnessing
[14] Leviathan: spirit twisting communication
[15] Cain: spirit stealing inheritance

CHAPTER 14
OVERCOMING TRAUMA AND BROKENNESS

'He has redeemed my soul from going to the pit, and my life shall see the light.'
(Job 33:28, NASB)

In 1 John 5:5, the Overcomer is the one who believes that Jesus is the son of God. Those who truly belong to Christ, who believe and abide in Him, are overcomers. They overcome the world because they believe God and have faith in Him.

Have you heard people excuse their sin, by saying this is who I am, and this is what my family does? They believe the lie of the enemy that they cannot change. They are not putting their faith in the One who overcame at the cross and in the grave. When we believe in Jesus as Lord, and the work He did on the cross for each one of us, we can abide in Him, and we can overcome.

> *Then I heard a loud voice in heaven, "Now salvation, and strength, and the kingdom of our God, and the power of His Christ have come, for the accuser of our brethren, who accused them before our God day and night, has been cast down. And they overcame him by the blood of the Lamb and by the word of their testimony, and they did not love their lives to the death."*
> *(Revelation 12:10-11, NKJV)*

An Overcomer is one that lives a victorious life and not defeated. There are three keys to overcome. First we overcome by the blood of the Lamb. In heaven's court, the blood has a voice. We see that the blood of Abel cried out when he was murdered by his brother. In the heavenly court, we bring the accusations of the accuser coming against us. We repent and renounce, break all agreement with the sin, lies, and disobedience to the word of God. We repent for opening the door to the spirit by trading with it either personally or generationally. Then we thank Jesus that His blood washes away the sin, the curse and over powers the accuser's voice. As a priest, we wash the sin, people, and situations with the blood of Jesus. When we come into the court of heaven, we have the legal right through the blood of Jesus Christ, to enter a plea and lay claim, to the evidence of His blood that was shed, and to his slain body to neutralize the power of sin, affliction, death and hell. We overcome by the blood.

Second, we overcome by the words of our testimony. What are you saying, thinking and agreeing with? You have the power to bless or curse with your tongue. Can you renounce the gossip, backbiting, putting others and yourself down? We believers are all part of the body of Christ. When you come against a member of the body, you are hurting yourself. Stop trading on trading floor so you can be an overcomer in Christ.

Third, we overcome by not loving our own lives unto death. The Passion Translation says we triumph:

> *"They conquered him completely through the blood of the Lamb and the powerful word of his testimony. They triumphed because they did not love and cling to their own lives, even when faced with death." (Rev. 12:11, TPT)*

We offer ourselves as a living sacrifice unto the Lord. We love our bodies as the temple of the Holy Spirit, and nurture our bodies, but we love Him more. We yield our will and agendas to Him. In ascension prayer, we see what the Father is doing so we can come into agreement with it.

The enemy is a roaring lion seeking to devour with the purpose to kill, steal, and destroy. We give the enemy legal right to come against us by trading with the enemy, by sinning and by generational curses.

DOUBLE MINDED; DIVIDED SOUL

When stress, trauma or abuse happens, people tend to dissociate, shut down, or just not remember. Many people will say, "I just don't remember my childhood". Under stress, parts of your soul may agree (trade) with the enemy in order to keep you functioning. Often the parts takes over as a protector so you can function as if nothing happened. But every now and then the part may get triggered by something happening in everyday life. In other words, the event happening today seems much greater, and you may go into a spin. The reason is because the soul part in the pit got activated. The Bible speaks of pits and how our soul can go to a pit (Job 33:18, 22, 24, 28-30).

Soul parts going to the pit is a real condition, and it can be serious enough to cause a person to split, and have a mental disorder, "Dissociative Identity Disorder" (DID) characterized by having at least two distinct personality states. People can become depressed; suffer from borderline personality or post-traumatic stress disorder due to this condition.

Through a dream, in 2009, the Lord gave me a key to healing Dissociative Identity Disorder through a dream. In the dream, I was in an elementary school classroom, listening to an instructor teach on DID, and I received the key of healing the disorder from Jesus. I ran down the hall to tell the instructor who left the classroom, and I couldn't find him. Instead, I was called into a classroom that was filled with people waiting for a doctor. To my surprise, all the patients had DID, and I was the doctor who they were waiting to see. The appointments I was told were scheduled only 15 minutes apart. That meant to me that God could heal this condition in only 15 minutes! While in Australia, in 2009 while ministering to a young man, who was severely fragmented, I got to facilitate his healing as literally, God put Humpty Dumpty back together again. Since this experience, I have seen God rescue people time and time again from the pit.

There can be several types of pits. David describes multiple pits in the Psalms (Ps. 28:1; 30:3, 9; 40:2; 143:7). There can be pits of fear, depression, and pits of being stuck.

We work with the soul part that is stuck, and often we are talking to a much younger version of the person. Gently we speak to the younger one to agree to allow Jesus to rescue the part, so it can come back. The client may see or sense himself/herself in a closet, in a cage, or any number of places. Once the part has made itself known, and is agreeable to letting go of the pit to go to Jesus, healing can come. It is essential that the client knows the part is with Jesus, so we can pray that healing over the wounded part. Often we see the part getting new clothes, coming back to life. We also pray that God brings the part to maturity washed in the blood. Once the part is mature, and is well, we ask Jesus, when is the part to come back to the client? It could be immediate or later. The important point is that the part does need to come back, so the person can become whole.

Much of our self-sabotaging behavior is because our core is not in alignment. That means that part of us wants to do something, and another part of us wants to do something different. So we are not in agreement with ourselves. We have internal conflicts. In 1 Corinthians 12:12, Paul states that the body is one. We may state, "I want to go after my vision, but part of me doesn't. I keep self-sabotaging myself." God wants us in alignment so we are not divided. We are to love Him, with all of our heart, soul and mind. The following is a tool I have used effectively and have adapted it to heal people of trauma. As outlined below, the tool can be used to move beyond stuck thinking.

CHAPTER 15: PICTURE IN PICTURE PIP — CORE ALIGNMENT

Where there is no vision, the people perish: but he that keepeth the law, happy is he.
(Prov. 29:18, KJV)

PICTURE IN PICTURE PIP

This life coaching method is a simple and powerful approach to assist clients to move beyond their current way of thinking, and experience a new possibility. I have adapted a tool to use to bring those who have suffered trauma into wholeness, changing the neural pathways of the negative experience in the brain.

CURRENT STATE + COACHING EXPERIENCE = DESIRED STATE

The basic coaching methodology is simple. We start where the client is in his current state. Second, define the desired state, and move the client to the completion of a goal or even beyond the completion of the goal. The vehicle or coach is what moves the client between the current state and the desired state. The coaching model is all about getting the client from where they are to where they want to be.

RESOURCES

1. Past Peak Experiences

Coaches can certainly use a client's past to assist with creating a powerful outcome, and future. The best way to do this is to search a client's past for resources, lessons learned, and examples of positive states of being. A client, who states they need confidence to take on a future situation and achieve an outcome, can be asked to remember a time when they were really confident. A simple question, like, "What is the moment in your life when you experienced the strongest sensation of confidence?" We all have strong positive memories of many resourceful and useful states of being that we can tap into, and "map across". Mapping across is simply applying a resourceful state, capability, skill, or behavior to a different environment.

2. Just Imagine

Our imagination can be one of our greatest assets. Our mind-brain system is capable of powerful imaginations. Just try for yourself: What would it feel like to fly like a bird? None of us have ever actually flown by simply flapping our arms, but we can imagine what the sensation might be like.

3. Mentor or Example

As a client is seeking to achieve a state we can simply ask them to think of a person who is good at the state they are trying to achieve. It can be someone they know personally, someone they are simply familiar with, a historical figure, or even a fictional character.

PIP TOOL

1. **Picture the vision** – What do you see? Is this how you want it? See it on the movie screen. Dissociate. Watch yourself on the screen.

2. **In – Step into the vision** – How do you stand? Move? How does that feel? How do you speak to yourself? Associate. You are now in the vision. From this future position, tell the present you how you got to the ideal future position. Note the steps.

3. **Picture** – Come back to the present. What were the most important action steps might you take to get to the ideal future vision? Dissociate.

TRAUMA TOOL

In 2011, while in Ecuador, I found out that children from a church school had been abused. I asked to be taken to the school, and found myself with a group of about 8 children, ages 5-10 years old, who had been severely abused. I was able to modify the above tool to bring healing to them. I asked them to draw a picture of what happened. They had pictures of the abusers, the ones that hurt them. Carlos's picture showed a big devil, in blue. I asked him where was God in this picture? Carlos drew a small dot in the corner. As a group, I asked them to imagine watching T.V. (they had never been to the movies). They were sitting on a couch with Jesus, and they replayed the event, watching it on T.V. We changed the color to black and white to remove the intensity. We changed the sounds from violent screams to a song, such as Jesus loves me.

They were able to take the blood of Jesus and watch the memory, removing the pain, hurt, and sounds. Then they were to watch the movie backwards. Each child practiced playing the film in reverse. After about three times, seven were not able pull up the memory anymore. God had removed the trauma, and they could go to Jesus. They drew a picture on the backside of their papers, that showed they were with Jesus and the perpetrators were very small or not on the papers.

I noticed Carlos on the floor crawling around the room unable to participate. I asked to be taken into a separate room with Carlos, and in English, I commanded all spirits coming against him to leave. Carlos was able to sit in a chair, and we went through the same process. He received the love of Jesus, and even drew a picture of sitting in Jesus' lap. I asked where the men that abused him were. He drew a small dot in the corner.

This tool shows how powerful our brain is. If we can imagine it, we can have it. God knows your imagination is powerful, and he wants to unlock your imagination to see, to think bigger. Imagination is the seed, the blank check of faith. If you can see it, you can have it. Imagination unlocks the potential, and it is when you are most like God. God is the Creator, and He is inviting you to partner with Him, to dream and co-create with Him.

What you focus on, you empower, and create to happen. It can be good or bad. What are you imagining? "What Job feared, came upon him." We can open the door to fear, and the worst can come like it did to Job. You know people that like to prepare themselves for the worst, and sure enough the worst happens. To be resourceful, we break agreement with lofty speculation, fear and chaos, coming out of negative spins, swirls, mindsets, limiting beliefs, and allow ourselves to partner with God and dream with Him. God commands us to renew our minds in Christ.

The intent of the heart brings desire, which brings fulfillment. What you think upon, meditate upon, and declare comes to pass. Another example is a couple in California, Bill and Kathy, who wanted children, but the doctor told them that they couldn't have children. Kathy had several miscarriages, but Bill wouldn't accept the diagnosis. He found a picture in a magazine of a father and a blond haired little girl around 4 years old with a pink bathing suit, and yellow swim fins standing by a pool. Bill took this picture, laid it out before the Lord, and prayed declaring that God would give them a child. God did give them a child, and years later, they took a vacation to an ocean side resort, and the wife took some pictures of her husband and daughter. After getting home, Bill looked at the pictures, and found a picture that was almost identical to the one he had cut out from the magazine and prayed over. The girl age 5 was in a pick bathing suit and was holding yellow swim fins and she and her father were standing by the ocean.

Finally, brethren, whatever things are true, whatever things are noble, whatever things are just, whatever things are pure, whatever things are lovely, whatever things are of good report, if there is any virtue and if there is anything praiseworthy—meditate on these things. (Phil 4:8, NKJV)

You will also declare a thing, and it will be established for you; so light will shine on your ways. (Job 22:28, NKJV)

For as he thinks in his heart, so is he. "Eat and drink!" he says to you, but his heart is not with you. (Prov. 23:7, NKJV)

I pray that the light of God will illuminate the eyes of your imagination, flooding you with light, until you experience the full revelation of the hope of his calling—that is, the wealth of God's glorious inheritances that he finds in us, his holy ones! (Eph. 1:18, TPT)

HOW THE TOOL WORKS

In dissociation, we take ourselves out of the picture, and observe the event from a distance. This is especially useful when someone has had trauma in their lives since they are reliving the trauma over and over. We can use the neocortex part of the brain, to make an image that is adjustable, taking the person out of the negative spin. In association, when we are in the memory, we feel the pain of the trauma, and the image is to adjust. When people have been traumatized, I ask them to put the image on a movie screen (dissociate) to separate from it. When it is on the screen, and they are in a safe place, with Jesus, the image can be washed with the blood, and changed. We can change the color, and sound, of the traumatic event, and in doing so, the neural pathways and response to the trauma can be changed.

When imagining, the brain fires almost 90% of the same neurology as actually participating. For example, Mary Lou Reton and other Olympians have imagined their success long before winning the gold medals. By imagining yourself doing, or even watching others, you are creating pathways and building neurology in your brain. This is true for the negative as well as the positive. For example, this is how porn can become addicting and the enemy uses our imagination to entrap us. On the other hand, we can use the imagination center to create the outcome and new habit systems that we want, in order to live a fulfilled life. Test the image. Is this how you want it to be? If not, you can change it. Then imagine what you do want.

CHAPTER 16 BECOMING AN OVERCOMER

"Then I heard a loud voice in heaven, "Now salvation, and strength, and the kingdom of our God, and the power of His Christ have come, for the accuser of our brethren, who accused them before our God day and night, has been cast down "And they overcame him by the blood of the Lamb and by the word of their testimony, and they did not love their lives to the death."
Rev. 12:10-11, NKJV)

OVERCOMERS

In 1 John 5:5, the overcomer is the one who believes that Jesus is the son of God. Those who truly belong to Christ, who believe and abide in Him, are overcomers. An overcomer is one that lives a victorious life and not defeated. There are three keys to overcome.

First we overcome by the blood of the Lamb. In heaven's court, the blood has a voice. We see that the blood of Abel cried out when he was murdered by his brother. In the heavenly court, we bring the accusations of the accuser coming against us. We repent and renounce, break all agreement with the sin, lies, and disobedience to the word of God. We repent for opening the door to the spirit by trading with it either personally or generationally. Then we thank Jesus that His blood washes away the sin, the curse and over powers the accuser's voice. As a priest, we wash the sin, people, and situations with the blood of Jesus. When we come into the court of heaven, we have the legal right through the blood of Jesus Christ, to enter a plea and lay claim to the evidence of His shed blood and slain body to neutralize the power of sin, affliction, death and hell. We overcome by the blood.

Second, we overcome by the words of our testimony. What are you saying, thinking and agreeing with? You have the power to bless or curse with your tongue. Can you renounce the gossip, backbiting, putting others and yourself down? We believers are all part of the body of Christ. When you come against a member of the body, you are hurting yourself. Stop trading on ungodly trading floors so you can be an overcomer in Christ.

Third, we overcome by not loving our own lives unto death. The Passion Translation states, "They triumphed because they did not love and cling to their own lives, even when faced with death." We offer ourselves as a living sacrifice unto the Lord. We love our bodies as the temple of the Holy Spirit, and nurture our bodies, but we love Him more. We yield our will and agendas to Him. In ascension prayer, we see what the Father is doing so we can come into agreement with it.

CHAPTER 17
PROMISES TO OVERCOMERS

"'He who has an ear, let him hear what the Spirit says to the churches. To him who overcomes I will give to eat from the tree of life, which is in the midst of the Paradise of God.'"

"'He who has an ear, let him hear what the Spirit says to the churches. He who overcomes shall not be hurt by the second death.'"

"'He who has an ear, let him hear what the Spirit says to the churches. To him who overcomes I will give some of the hidden manna to eat. And I will give him a white stone, and on the stone a new name written which no one knows except him who receives it."

And he who overcomes, and keeps My works until the end, to him I will give power over the nations—
(Rev. 2:7, 11, 17, 26; NKJV)

He who overcomes shall be clothed in white garments, and I will not blot out his name from the Book of Life; but I will confess his name before My Father and before His angels.

He who overcomes, I will make him a pillar in the temple of My God, and he shall go out no more. I will write on him the name of My God and the name of the city of My God, the New Jerusalem, which comes down out of heaven from My God. And I will write on him My new name.

To him who overcomes I will grant to sit with Me on My throne, as I also overcame and sat down with My Father on His throne.
(Rev. 3: 5, 12, 21; NKJV)

PROMISES TO THE SEVEN CHURCHES

1. **Ephesus (Rev. 2:1-7)**

   ### What We Are To Overcome

   Losing our first love – Though the Ephesians were doctrinally sound, persevered trials, and did not tolerate false teaching, they were losing their passionate love for Christ. We are to resist allowing people, things, and circumstances to get in our way of our intimate relationship with the Lord. The Lord commands them to return to their first love.

   ### Promises to Overcomer

   To the overcomer, the one who puts Jesus first, the Lord gives access to feast on the fruit of the tree of life found in the paradise of God (Rev. 2:7).

   ### Loss By Not Overcoming

   By allowing complacency to overtake passion, one becomes dull, and loses their lampstand, their light and place of influence for Jesus (Isa. 60:1). A second loss would be the impartation of the seven spirits of the Lord: the spirit of the Lord, the spirit of wisdom, the spirit of understanding, the spirit of counsel, the spirit of might, the spirit of knowledge, and the spirit of the fear of the Lord, since the lampstand also represents the seven spirits of God (Isa. 11:2-3).

   ### Parallels

   The overcomer may eat of the tree of life, bearing fruit every season, with leaves that heal the nations (Rev. 22:2).

2. **Smyrna (Rev. 2:8-11)**

   ### What We Are To Overcome

   Overcome suffering, and the fear of suffering, slander, and accusations.

   ### Promises to Overcomer

   To the overcomer, the Lord gives the Victor's Crown of Life, and you will overcome the second death.

   ### Loss By Not Overcoming

   They will succumb to the second death.

Parallels

The overcomer will be blessed, holy, priests of God, and will reign with Christ for a thousand years (Rev. 20:6).

3. ## Pergamum (Rev. 2:12-17)

   ### What We Are To Overcome

   Allowing false doctrine to come in, compromising the truth, the word of God. Holding on to false teachings of Balaam and Nicolaitans; tradition instead of the word of God.

   ### Promises to Overcomer

   To the overcomer, you will receive discernment, knowing truth from error, and feast upon hidden manna. You will know your identity in Christ, and you'll be given a white stone with a new name on it.

   ### Loss By Not Overcoming

   By not overcoming, the Lord will fight against you with the sword in His mouth.
   ### Parallels

   To the overcomer, you will drink from the spring of water of life without cost. You will receive an inheritance as a son. You will become a living stone making up the New Jerusalem (Rev. 21:6, 7, 11).

4. ## Thyatira (Rev. 2:18-29)

   ### What We Are To Overcome

   Tolerating and partnering with the spirit of Jezebel, who comes against the prophetic, and leads His bondservants astray through immorality and sacrificing to idols, and teaches witchcraft and the deep Satanic secrets. You overcome by holding fast.

   ### Promises to Overcomer

   To the overcomer, you will be given authority over nations; you will shepherd and rule them with a royal scepter; you will be given the Morning Star.

   ### Loss By Not Overcoming

   Those partnering with the spirit of Jezebel, will become sick, suffer tribulation, and have their children killed.

   ### Parallels

   Jesus is the bright Morning Star (Rev. 22:16).

5. **Sardis (Rev. 3:1-6)**

   ### What We Are To Overcome

   Dead Church focuses on works instead of faith. Works were incomplete. Wake up. Remember what you've received. Hear, and obey.

   ### Promises to Overcomer

   To the overcomer, who remains pure, the Lord will dress him in white and never blot out his name from the book of life, but will acknowledge his name before His father and His angels. He will walk in fellowship with the Lamb, the brilliant light and be called worthy; (Rev. 21:23-24).

   ### Loss By Not Overcoming

   Lose identity in Christ by putting identity in works and reputation.

   > *And then I will declare to them, "I never knew you; depart from Me, you who practice lawlessness." (Matt. 7:23, NKJV)*

   ### Parallels

   He calls you worthy, so receive it. The overcomer will gain entry into the city which is only for those whose names are in the Book of Life (Rev. 21:27).

6. **Philadelphia (Rev. 3:7-13)**

   ### What We Are To Overcome

   Denying Jesus and letting the enemy steal our crowns.

   ### Promises to Overcomer

   You will be a pillar in the sanctuary of God and secure. He will write on you the name of God and the city name of God, New Jerusalem. You will be kept from testing.

   ### Loss By Not Overcoming

   Lose Crowns; Loss of open doors of opportunity, favor, & fullness.

   ### Parallels

   New Jerusalem is descending. New Jerusalem contains the bridal DNA; the bride is being prepared for her husband; God is tabernacling with human beings (Rev. 21: 2-3).

7. **Laodicea (Rev. 3:14-22)**

   ### What We Are To Overcome

   Being lukewarm, neither hot nor cold, neither fervent nor frozen, being rich but spiritually poor, being miserable, blind, barren, & naked. Buy from Him gold refined with fire, white garments, & eye salve to see. Allow him to take the fig leafs off and unmask you.

   ### Promises to Overcomer

   You will be granted to sit with Him on His throne. And you shall be priests with God & reign forever & ever.

   ### Loss By Not Overcoming

   Lose white robe to clothe shame. Adam was naked and covered himself with a fig leaf; Loss of vision.

   ### Parallels

   The saints and the martyrs will rule with Christ 1,000 years (Rev. 20:4, 6; 22:5).

CHAPTER 18 — HOW TO OVERCOME

I have been crucified with Christ; it is no longer I who live, but Christ lives in me; and the life which I now live in the flesh I live by faith in the Son of God, who loved me and gave Himself for me.
(Gal. 2:20, NKJV)

HOW DO WE OVERCOME?

I purpose that we overcome by position and not by discipline. We overcome by re-garmenting. We take off the old and put on the new as in chapter 11, the Divine Exchange. We position ourselves in Christ. (Eph. 1:4, 6, 9, 10, 12, 20, 23; 2:6, 10, 13). When we are in Him, in Christ Jesus, we live, move, and have our being (Acts 17:28). So by taking off the old, we put on the new. We are new creations in Christ.

In order to move forward, and walk in the authority given to us by Christ, we surrender to Him as a Living Sacrifice, and enter into Christ, putting Him on. We no longer are operating under discipline and self-control, bridling our flesh, but are operating by becoming one with Christ, as we co-union with Christ. When we put on the armor of God in Ephesians 6, and His righteousness, we are actually putting on Christ. We are putting on the armor of light. Darkness is displaced by light. We become light. It is no longer we who live, but Christ who is living in us, and having His being in us. We become absorbed by who He is. We become light beings, going back to who we were before the fall of man. We let Him fight the battles. All we have to do is stand in Christ after putting on the armor of God. (Eph 6)

CHAPTER 19 PUTTING ON THE MIND OF CHRIST

For "who has known the mind of the Lord, that he will instruct him?"
But we have the mind of Christ.
(1 Cor. 2:16, NKJV)

PUT ON THE MIND OF CHRIST.

Are you achieving the desired outcomes and success that you want? If you sense that there is more that God has more you and you haven't been able to reach your potential, you may consider evaluating your thinking.

> *For as he thinks in his heart, so is he. "Eat and drink!" he says to you, but his heart is not with you. (Prov. 23:7, NKJV)*

Inside, you may have thoughts or beliefs that success is not attainable for you, and you are powerless and victimized as the events of your life spiral out of control. But what does God say?

> *For I know the thoughts that I think toward you, says the Lord, thoughts of peace and not of evil, to give you a future and a hope. (Jer. 29:11, NKJV)*

Transformation comes by Renewing your Mind in Christ Jesus. Every thought you have is from the kingdom of darkness or from the kingdom of light. By meditating on a thought, you are either partnering with the kingdom of darkness or with the kingdom of light.

> *For the weapons of our warfare are not of the flesh, but divinely powerful for the destruction of fortresses. We are destroying speculations and every lofty thing raised up against the knowledge of God, and we are taking every thought captive to the obedience of Christ. (2 Cor. 10:4, 5, NASB)*

The way we think rules our life. Our mindset is either a fortress, a stronghold, for the enemy, or a temple for the living God. A stronghold of the enemy acts as a filter keeping the truth of God from coming in. Without the strongholds, our mind can be a temple, a habitation for the living God. The Holy Spirit transforms us to a new way of thinking that empowers obedience. The enemy comes to steal, kill, and destroy, but Jesus came that we may have life, and life abundantly (John 10:10). We can move from scarcity to abundance by transforming our minds in Christ.

By partnering with the Holy Spirit, speculations can be pulled down. Speculations are the way we look at things outwardly, through the lens of fear, surmising, condemnation, doctrines, opinions, and judgments. The Holy Spirit can remove the scales on the eyes enabling us to see without these lenses that keep us from embracing the truth and the freedom God has for us. Saul who was persecuting Christians had a major lens change when he was blinded by the light of Jesus, and met his Savior whom he has been persecuting (Acts 9). By judging and condemning others, one is actually partnering with the accuser of the brethren and moved by a religious spirit and not by the Holy Spirit. When the scales are removed, the Holy Spirit restores our confidence in Christ so we can look at issues from the inner man of the spirit.

To have fellowship with God, we have to think like Him, and put on the mind of Christ, seeing the future, moving from present to future, instead of being focused on past events and trauma. We are to move from glory to glory being transformed into the image of Christ (2 Cor. 3:18).

You have the mind of Christ. What does that mean? Why are so many Christians struggling and not able to overcome the enemy in their lives? There can be generational legal rights of the enemy to harass us, but must we live under the tyranny of our ancestor's and our sins?

I don't believe so. Through prayer, we can break free from our ancestor's sins, and break agreement with ungodly beliefs that have kept us earth bound. Ephesians 1-2 states than we are in Christ Jesus and seated in heavenly places presently. We don't have to wait until we die, but our spirit man is already in heaven. So, if we are seated with Christ in the heavenlies, why are we still earthbound?

The answer is in coming into agreement with God's perspective of who you are, and not the enemy's perspective. Where is your focus? What you put your attention on, you create in your life. If your attention is on the old nature, then you are resurrecting that which Christ died for. If you put your attention on who you are in Christ and change your perspective to see yourself as He sees you, you are being made into His image. This is who Christ is returning for: a pure bride without spot or wrinkle.

Paul prayed in Ephesians 1:18 for a lens change. Paul had experienced a lens change in his encounter with the Light of the world. He prays that the eyes of your heart may be illuminated.

I pray that the eyes of your heart may be enlightened, so that you will know what is the hope of His calling, what are the riches of the glory of His inheritance in the saints, and what is the surpassing greatness of His power toward us who believe. These are in accordance with the working of the strength of His might which He brought about in Christ, when He raised Him from the dead and seated Him at His right hand in the heavenly places, far above all rule and authority and power and dominion, and every name that is named, not only in this age but also in the one to come. And He put all things in subjection under His feet, and gave Him as head over all things to the church, which is His body, the fullness of Him who fills all in all.

But God, being rich in mercy, because of His great love with which He loved us, even when we were dead in our transgressions, made us alive together with Christ (by grace you have been saved), and raised us up with Him, and seated us with Him in the heavenly places in Christ Jesus, so that in the ages to come He might show the surpassing riches of His grace in kindness toward us in Christ Jesus. (Eph. 1:18-23; 2:4-6)

What you meditate on, focus on, you create, and empower. What you think upon, you breathe life upon, creating it to happen. Negativity is a speculation. If you think upon the negative and past circumstances, you become stuck, unable to move forward. For example, stress is not caused by external circumstances but by the way you perceive of the circumstances. You have the power to open the door to stress and anxiety or not. The result of focusing on the negative is stress and anxiety. God is restoring our thinking and renewing our minds in Christ.

Therefore, if anyone is in Christ, he is a new creation; old things have passed away; behold, all things have become new. (2 Cor. 5:17, NKJV)

Our new nature is the way God thinks of us. Our old nature is a product of our placement in the world. Our new nature is a product of our placement in heaven. Ephesians 2 states we are seated with Christ in heavenly places. In times of stress, there is a tendency to focus on the worst, taking in doubt, unbelief, fear, and anxiety. By going over and over the negative, it's possible for one to go into a downward spin causing him/her to be stuck in a pit, unable to get out without help.

You cannot serve two masters. You are either serving the serving the kingdom of light or the kingdom of darkness by agreement. The Lord wants to bring you into alignment with His sound, frequency, color, light and vibration. You have a receiver like a satellite dish. You are tuning into the frequency of life or to the frequency of death. There were two trees in the garden: the tree of life and the tree of the knowledge of good and evil. When Eve agreed with the lies of the enemy to doubt and not trust that God had superior purpose and intention for her, she opened the door and accepted an inferior scroll and destiny for her and her seed.

God has a future and a hope for you. God already has your success, prosperity and fulfillment planned out for you. Your divine birthright that God had for you in the beginning is good. Often the enemy intercepts the divine birthright by accosting your spirit to come into agreement with his plan instead of God's plan at a very young age. Your divine birthright given by God can actually be sabotaged by agreement with the enemy's plan through generational sin, rejection, fear, or through life events when you are a child, in the womb, or even on the way to conception. But thank God that we do not have to remain in that state.

CHAPTER 20
TAKING TERRITORY

For all the land which you see, I will give it to you and to your descendants forever.
(Gen. 13:15 NASB)

First as a priest, we take territory for Christ within ourselves. The father's desire is to tabernacle within us. When we are in Christ and have received the Holy Spirit, we become temples of the Father, Son, and Holy Spirit. As we yield to Christ, and renounce the ungodly trading of our family lines and ourselves, Satan loses his hold and hook in us.

Individuals may house demons and territorial spirits as in Mark 5:8-10, when Jesus encountered a demon possessed man. Its name was Legion, meaning many, so it's possible to suggest that this man housed territorial principalities for the region. When he was delivered, the region was able to receive Christ. When the 70 were sent by Jesus to cast out demons, Jesus saw Satan falling from heaven like lightning (Luke 10:17-20). This is a key to taking regions for Christ. As people get delivered, territorial spirits lose their grasps, and light can displace darkness. When principalities fall like lightning over a city and no longer rule the minds of people, it is imperative that Kingdom authority replace these fallen princes. This is why as priests we renounce and forgive people and creation that has partnered with evil to set territories free. We wash with the blood of the lamb, and replace the evil with good. We replace the ungodly territorial spirits with God's angels to govern the land.

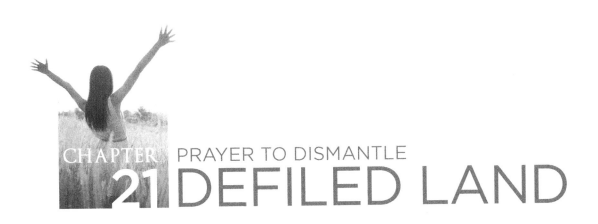

CHAPTER 21
PRAYER TO DISMANTLE DEFILED LAND

"Arise, walk about the land through its length and breadth; for I will give it to you."
(Gen. 13:17, NASB)

Prayer to Dismantle Defiled Land by Scott Norvell

Father, we ask You to give us our daily bread of revelation and freedom for the city of _____. We ask You to anoint us for this work of dismantling all infrastructure of evil and establishing Your rule in this city. We ask You to shine Your Light on this city that the hidden sins committed across all time on this land will be revealed. We commit to taking the time, however long it is, to walking out the process of sanctification that You lead us through. We call upon You Lord Jesus, Lion of the Tribe of Judah to come to this place and roar, establishing Your dominion on earth as it is in heaven. We wait upon You Lord to show us what root sins need to be forgiven this day.

We forgive every person you are highlighting to us as having sinned in this city, and thus defiled the land. We forgive every person of influence and authority in the city. We forgive every servant in the community, especially those responsible for executive, legislative and judicial / enforcement duties. We forgive every resident and all those who have visited the area. We forgive all persons that we have been in covenant with and all those that have trespassed against us. We receive and wash their feet with the Blood of Jesus that the power of our sins is broken. All curses are broken. All defilement: all bloodshed, broken covenant, idolatry, and all sexual immorality is washed away. All wounds are healed. Everything false is revealed in the Light and forgiven. All vows, oaths, or covenants of evil are dissolved. And all witchcraft, manipulation, and control is dismantled, unraveled, undone, and rendered powerless. We are purified of all unrighteousness, and redeemed of every consequence. We hurl down the accuser with the Blood of the Lamb and the word of our testimony. The demonic stronghold is unplugged and shut down.

I bind and cast all demons that have just lost their rights to torment or afflict to the feet of Jesus, and tell them never to return. All conspiracies are thwarted. All portals, gates, doors, or windows of evil are shut. All demonic blockades at the gates of this city are demolished and removed. We ask You Father to come, All Consuming Fire, and burn all residue of evil out of the city of _____. We post all angels assigned to _____ in their respective positions. Through our choice of unity and purity from the Blood of the Lamb, we call these angels fully clothed and armed with every resource that they will need to complete their assignments. Father, I ask You to bless _____ with peace, joy, happiness, and the favor of God. Amen.

ABOUT THE AUTHOR

 **Dale Shannon,** a Christian Life Purpose Coach, directs Fulfill Your Dream ministry created to empower and equip individuals to discover and fulfill their God given dreams, life purposes and desired outcomes. Her passion is releasing people into fullness to overcome both obstacles and limiting beliefs, and through the renewing of their minds in Christ (Romans 12:2), transform the way they perceive, think, speak, and act. Dale and her husband Doug, have two children and five grandchildren.

Made in the USA
Columbia, SC
19 October 2018